GIMME FIVE!

GIMME FIVE!

**Recipes, tips and inspiring ideas for
enticing your child to eat and enjoy
fruits and vegetables**

NICOLA GRAIMES

Carroll & Brown Publishers Limited

First published in 2005 in the United Kingdom by

Carroll & Brown Publishers Limited
20 Lonsdale Road
London NW6 6RD

Food Stylist Clare Lewis
Photographer Jules Selmes
Assistant David Yems

Text © Nicola Graimes 2005
Illustrations and compilation © Carroll & Brown Limited 2005

A CIP catalogue record for this book is available from the British Library.

ISBN 1-904760-11-2

10 9 8 7 6 5 4 3 2 1

Reproduced by RDC, Malaysia
Printed and bound in Hong Kong by Everbest

CONTENTS

Introduction

This book is the result of many conversations with other mums about how difficult it is to get children to eat fruits and vegetables. I can't promise miracles but the best tips from these conversations – practical, fun and sometimes sneaky ideas – are used in this book.

How much is enough?

We all know that eating plenty of fruits and vegetables makes us healthier and potentially live longer. What's more, most of us are familiar with the "five-a-day" guidelines initiated by the World Health Organization and supported by health bodies and governments around the world. Yet this amount is now seen by many countries as a minimum recommendation. Dr Lorelei di Sogra, director of the five-a-day campaign for the American National Cancer Institute, says that they currently recommend the ideal minimum of five

TOP TEN TIPS

These are the most popular suggestions given by parents.

1 *Blend fresh fruits – and even vegetables – into smoothies and shakes.*
2 *Make it fun: give a meal a theme and take time with presentation.*
3 *Liquidize vegetables and lentils or beans in a tomato pasta sauce.*
4 *Involve your children in the weekly shop.*
5 *Make up a big vegetable and bean soup and blend until smooth.*
6 *Get children involved in preparing and cooking a meal.*
7 *Raw vegetables – usually served as crudités – are often more popular than cooked.*
8 *Transform fruit into ice creams, mousses and fools.*
9 *Add extra veg to the most popular kid's meals such as burgers, pizza, mashed potatoes or pies.*
10 *Start the day well: a glass of fresh fruit juice and cereal topped with chopped fruit for breakfast will make it easier to achieve the recommended daily five.*

vegetable, for children the recommended amount is less obvious. I find the most practical measure is that a portion equals the amount a child can fit in one hand; as the child grows, so does the portion size. To make this easier, *Gimme 5* details how many portions of fresh produce each recipe provides per person. The recipes have been developed to feed four people – two adults, two children.

portions for children, seven for women and nine for men. Other countries recommend ten portions. In reality, however, many of us barely manage to eat three portions a day, often less.

What's all the fuss about?

Are fruits and vegetables really as important as the experts claim? The answer is an overwhelming yes, especially with the growing incidence of obesity, diabetes, cancer and heart disease among not just adults but children too. Dieticians believe that eating a minimum of five portions of fruits and vegetables each day could help prevent an impressive 20 per cent of deaths from the biggest killer diseases in the West.

What's a portion?

Many parents say the most difficult part of implementing the five-a-day recommendation is knowing what constitutes a portion. For adults, a portion is 80 g or 3 oz of any given fruit or

Start young

Our eating habits and dietary preferences are formed in the first few years of life, so ideally children should enjoy a wide range of foods as early as possible. But don't panic: I know children who have lived on little more than jam sandwiches for weeks on end and now happily eat a healthy, varied diet. It's never too late to start. The goal of this book is to encourage a love of good "real" food.

Why five?

Fruits and vegetables are classified by dieticians as "nutrient dense". This means that they provide a high ratio of vitamins and minerals in relation to the calories they contain. What's more, they are generally low in fat, rich in antioxidants and a good source of fibre.

The evidence supporting the benefits of a diet rich in fruits and vegetables is impressive. Research has found that eating at least five portions of different fruits and vegetables a day may reduce the risk of death from some chronic diseases by up to 20 per cent. A recent study found that increased intake of vegetables by just one portion a day may lower the risk of heart disease by 40 per cent and the risk of stroke by 6 per cent. Research shows

other benefits too, such as delay in the development of cataracts, reduction in the symptoms of asthma and improvement in bowel function.

Along with direct health benefits, eating fruits and vegetables can help to achieve other dietary goals, particularly those that are increasingly affecting children. By eating at least five portions a day, children increase their fibre intake and reduce their fat and sugar intake, all of which help to maintain a healthy weight.

The reason why fruits and vegetables are so beneficial is because they provide a wide range of plant nutrients known as phytochemicals as well as vitamins and minerals. Many of these nutrients are antioxidants, which are said to destroy

harmful free radicals in the body. These free radicals are known to play a role in causing cancer as well as other harmful side-effects.

Can I just take a pill?

Unfortunately it is not as simple as that. While nutritional supplements may help those on a restricted diet and those who show deficiencies in certain nutrients, they can't take the place of a balanced diet, rich in fruits and vegetables.

Research shows that the benefits of fresh produce derive not only from the individual vitamins and minerals, but how these work together in the body. Dietary supplements contain isolated vitamins and minerals that do not appear to provide the same health benefits and cannot replace the disease-fighting phytochemicals found in fruits and vegetables. The nutrients in fresh produce have been found to work in tandem in the body. For example, vitamin C-rich foods, such as oranges and lemons, can boost iron absorption in iron-rich green vegetables by up to 30 per cent. Vitamin C is also more potent when combined with bioflavanoids, plant chemicals found in blackberries, cherries, lemons, carrots, cabbage, lentils and oranges, amongst others, which are thought to prevent certain forms of cancer.

Latest research by the University of Illinois in America supports this theory. It found that a combination of broccoli and tomatoes eaten together may become the latest strategy in the

Good plant sources of vitamins and minerals
- *Vitamin C – citrus fruit, strawberries, kiwi fruit, berries, green vegetables, tomatoes, sprouted beans, papaya, peppers*
- *Vitamin A (beta-carotene) – carrots, pumpkins, apricots, mango, cantaloupe melon*
- *Vitamin E – avocado, sun-dried tomatoes, tomato purée*
- *B vitamins – lentils, beans, green vegetables, seaweed*
- *Calcium – green leafy vegetables, apricots, seaweed, beans*
- *Magnesium – green leafy vegetables, dried fruit, soya beans*
- *Iron – parsley, green vegetables, nori seaweed, lentils, beans, dried fruit, baked beans in tomato sauce*
- *Selenium – lentils, dried mushrooms*
- *Zinc – pulses, seaweed*

fight against some forms of cancer. Both vegetables are known to have cancer-fighting qualities, but scientists believe that it's the lycopene, which turns tomatoes red, and the glucosinolates in broccoli, that are responsible for these findings.

Vitamins & minerals

Vitamins and minerals are crucial for the production of energy, boosting the immune system, the nervous system – in fact, practically pretty much every body process.

Fruits and vegetables provide plentiful amounts of the antioxidants beta-carotene (a carotenoid that is converted to vitamin A in the body), vitamins C and E as well as certain B vitamins, including folic acid. Beta-carotene is the yellow-orange pigment found in such foods as carrots and pumpkin. Along with vitamin C, it plays a role in protecting our bodies from the damage caused by harmful free radicals that destroy cells and tissues and can lead to heart disease and cancers.

Pulses, dried fruit and green leafy vegetables provide a range of minerals, including calcium and iron. Children are particularly prone to iron deficiency, which can cause listlessness, poor concentration, behavioural problems and irritability.

Fibre

Fruits, vegetables and pulses are good sources of soluble fibre, which can help to reduce cholesterol levels, maintain healthy digestion and keep blood glucose levels steady and energy levels constant.

Antioxidants

As mentioned before, nutrients do not work in isolation, but rely

on the presence of others for their effectiveness. Many vitamins, minerals and phytochemicals are antioxidants, which work together to protect our bodies from the harmful effects of substances called free radicals, an excess of which may predispose us to cancer and heart disease.

Phytochemicals

Recent research has identified a number of natural plant compounds that could play a crucial role in preventing heart disease, diabetes and cancers, and these compounds may even in the future be classified as essential nutrients. There are literally hundreds of different phytochemicals found in plant foods and along with their numerous health benefits they are also responsible for the colour, smell and flavour of a fruit or vegetable. There is still much to learn about phyto-chemicals as they appear to help the body in a variety of ways, but one thing is certain: they are a vital part of good health.

The following examples are all phytochemicals (see Eat a Rainbow, pages 16–17, for where they can be found).

- **Carotenoids** – powerful antioxidants, protect against cancer and heart disease.
- **Bioflavanoids** – powerful antioxidants, stimulate the immune system, anti-inflammatory and protect against cancer.
- **Glucosinolates** – powerful detoxifiers, boost the immune system.
- **Phytoestrogens** – reduce the risk of hormone-dependent cancers such as breast and womb cancer.
- **Organosulphides** – anti-oxidants that stimulate the immune system.

Asthma research

Like other allergic conditions such as eczema and hayfever, asthma tends to run in families, although the number of children affected appears to be on the increase. Recent studies show a correlation between asthma and a diet lacking in fruits and vegetables. A diet that includes plenty of different types of fruits and vegetables has been shown to play a preventative role as well as relieving the severity of an attack by helping to open up the airways.

What's a Portion?

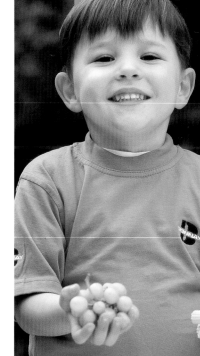

We all know that fruits and vegetables are good for us, yet most of us only eat about half the recommended daily amount. And, when it comes to fruits and vegetables and children, it can be hard to even come close. Getting your child to eat up his or her "greens" may be tricky, but tricky does not mean impossible.

The ratio of fruits to vegetables

The amount of fruit and vegetables a child needs is not the same as his or her parents. Health professionals recommend we all eat a minimum of five portions of fresh fruits and vegetables a day – adults should eat two fruits and three vegetables, while children should have three portions of fruit and two of vegetables. Children need the extra calories and energy that fruit provides over vegetables. It is also important the fruits and vegetables be as varied and colourful as possible. Differently coloured fruits and vegetables provide a range of nutrients, including vitamin C, folate, beta-carotene and fibre.

Portion sizes

The size of a child's portion also differs from that of an adult and is often much smaller than we think. As a general guide, a portion is the amount a child can hold in one hand and, as his or her hand grows, so should the size of the portion. For school-aged children, this is equivalent to around ½ cup per portion (a cup is the size of an average coffee mug).

Food source

You can choose from fresh, frozen, canned, dried or juiced fruits and vegetables, although the latter only counts as one portion a day no matter how much you drink.

Contrary to popular belief, frozen and canned often contain more nutrients than fresh, especially if the latter is more than five days old. Fruit and vegetables are frozen quickly after harvesting so they retain a high level of certain nutrients. When foods are canned they are exposed to high intensity heat which can make some nutrients, such as beta-carotene and lycopene, more usable by the body. Although dried fruit contains very little vitamin C compared to fresh, it is a richer source of iron and fibre. Ready-meals – usually vegetarian – and prepared salads, soups

What doesn't count?

Either because their starch content is too high or their fruit or vegetable content is too low, the following items do not count as a portion:

- *Potatoes, yams and sweet potatoes*
- *Fruit drinks, squashes or fruit-flavoured drinks*
- *Fruit yogurts*
- *Jams and marmalades*
- *Ketchup and the tomato sauce in baked beans*

and tomato-based pasta sauces also count, as long as they contain a high percentage of vegetables. To double check, look at the food label – those foods that feature at the top of the ingredients list are present in the highest quantity. Many food manufacturers now highlight the five-a-day logo on the packaging, indicating how many portions are provided. Watch out, though, as ready-made foods may also contain high levels of added salt, sugar and fat.

Daily quota

Ideally, the recommended minimum of five portions should be spread throughout the day, and for children this equates to three main meals and two snacks. This can be achieved, for instance, by serving:

- A glass of fresh fruit juice (not from concentrate or fruit drink) at breakfast
- A fruity snack
- A vegetable and bean soup for lunch, followed by a piece of fruit
- A fruity snack
- A vegetable pizza, pasta or rice dish, followed by a fruity dessert for pudding.

Accompany the soup with some vegetable crudités and humous dip and the supper with steamed vegetables or salad, and you can boost the five-a-day quota by another 2–3 portions.

The current guidelines on what constitutes a portion of fruit, vegetables or pulses are based on adult requirements and these can vary depending on which official figures you consult. For an adult, one portion is about 80 g or 3 oz. For children this amount is smaller – about a handful. The following figures are for children and are "educated estimates", while the larger quantities are based on UK Department of Health guidelines for adults.

PORTION SIZE
• However much you drink, fruit and vegetable juices and smoothies count as a maximum of one portion a day.

•• However much you eat, pulses count as a maximum of one portion a day.

FRUIT
Apple, dried rings, 1 handful or 2–4 rings
Apple, fresh, 1 small to medium
Apple, purée, 2 heaped tbsp
Apricot, canned, 4–6 halves
Apricot, fresh, 1–3
Apricot, dried, 1–3 whole
Avocado, ½
Banana chips, 1 handful
Banana, fresh, 1 small to medium
Blackberries, 1 handful or 9–10
Blackcurrants, 2–4 heaped tbsp
Blueberries, 1–2 handfuls or 2–4 heaped tbsp
Cherries, canned, 1 handful or 3 heaped tbsp or 11
Cherries, dried, 1 handful or 1 heaped tbsp
Cherries, fresh, 1 handful or 14
Clementines, fresh, 1–2
Currants, dried, 1 heaped tbsp
Dates, fresh, 2–3
Fig, dried, 1–2
Fig, fresh, 1–2
Fruit juice, 150 ml/5 fl oz glass•
Fruit salad, canned, 2–3 heaped tbsp
Fruit salad, fresh, 2–3 heaped tbsp
Fruit smoothie, 150 ml/5 fl oz glass•
Gooseberries, 1 handful
Grapefruit segments, canned, 2–3 heaped tbsp or 8 segments

VEGETABLES
Artichoke, 1–2 globe hearts
Asparagus, canned, 5–7 spears
Asparagus, fresh, 3–5 spears
Aubergine, 1 handful or ⅓ medium
Beans, French, 2–4 heaped tbsp
Beans, runner, 2–4 heaped tbsp
Beetroot, bottled, 2–3 "baby" whole, or 7 slices
Broccoli, 1–2 florets
Brussels sprouts, 4–8
Cabbage, sliced, 1–2 handfuls
Cabbage, shredded, 2–3 heaped tbsp
Carrots, canned, 2–3 heaped tbsp
Carrots, fresh, slices 2–3 heaped tbsp
Carrots, shredded, handful or ⅓ cereal bowl
Cauliflower, 1 handful or 4–8 florets
Celery, 1–3 sticks
Courgettes, 1 handful or ½ large
Cucumber, 5 cm/2 in piece
Curly kale, cooked, 2–4 heaped tbsp
Leeks, 1 small to medium (white portion only)
Lettuce (mixed leaves) 1 cereal bowl
Mangetout, 1 handful
Mixed vegetables, frozen, 2–3 tbsp
Mushrooms, button, 1 handful or sliced 2–4 heaped tbsp
Mushrooms, dried, 2 tbsp or handful porcini
Okra, 1 handful or 16 medium

Grapefruit, fresh, ½
Grapes, 1 handful
Kiwi fruit, 1–2
Lychees, fresh or canned, 4–6
Mandarin orange, canned, 2–3 heaped tbsp
Mandarin orange, fresh, 1 small to medium
Mango, 1–2 slices (5 cm/2 in slice)
Melon, 1 slice (5 cm/2 in slice)
Mixed fruit, dried, handful or 1 heaped tbsp
Nectarine, fresh, 1
Orange, fresh, 1
Papaya (pawpaw), fresh, 1 slice
Passion fruit, 4–6

Peach, canned, 2 halves or 7 slices
Peach, dried, 1–2 halves
Peach, fresh, 1 small to medium
Pear, canned, 2 halves or 7 slices
Pear, dried, 1–2 halves
Pear, fresh, 1 small to medium
Pineapple, canned, 1–2 rings or 12 chunks
Pineapple, crushed, 2–3 tbsp
Pineapple, dried, 1 heaped tbsp
Pineapple, fresh, 1 medium to large slice
Plum, 1–2 medium
Prune, canned, 4–6
Prune, dried, 2–3
Raisins, ½–1 heaped tbsp

Raspberries, canned, 1 handful or 20
Raspberries, fresh, 1–2 handfuls
Rhubarb, canned, 3–5 chunks
Rhubarb, cooked, 2 heaped tbsp
Satsuma, 1–2 small
Squash, 1 handful to 2 tbsp
Strawberry, fresh, 1 handful or 7
Sultanas, ½–1 heaped tbsp
Tangerine, 1–2 small

Onion, dried, 1 heaped tbsp
Onion, fresh, 1 handful or 1 medium
Parsnips, 1 medium to large
Peas, canned, 2–3 heaped tbsp
Peas, fresh, 2–3 heaped tbsp
Peas, frozen, 2–3 heaped tbsp
Pepper, fresh, 1 handful or ½
Pumpkin, 1 handful to 2 tbsp diced
Radish, 1 handful or 10
Spinach, cooked, 1–2 heaped tbsp
Spinach, fresh, 1 handful or 1 cereal bowl
Spring greens, cooked, 2–4 heaped tbsp
Spring onion, 1 handful or 8 onions
Sugarsnap peas, 1 handful
Swede, diced, 2–3 heaped tbsp

Sweetcorn, baby, 1 handful or 6 cobs
Sweetcorn, canned, 2–3 heaped tbsp
Sweetcorn, on the cob, ½–1
Tomato purée, 1 heaped tbsp
Tomato, canned plum, 1–2 whole
Tomato, fresh, 1 medium, or handful
Tomato, sun-dried, 2–4 pieces
Vegetable juice, 150 ml/5 fl oz glass•

PULSES ••
Beans, black eye, cooked, 1 handful or 2–3 heaped tbsp
Beans, broad, cooked, 1 handful or 2–3 heaped tbsp
Beans, butter, cooked, 1 handful or 2–3 heaped tbsp
Beans, cannellini, cooked, 1 handful or 2–3 heaped tbsp
Beans, kidney, cooked, 1 handful or 2–3 heaped tbsp
Bean sprouts, fresh, 1–2 handfuls
Chickpeas, cooked, 1 handful or 2–3 heaped tbsp
Lentils, 1 handful or 2–3 tbsp
Sprouted beans or lentils, 1 handful or 2–3 tbsp

Eat a rainbow ...

A good way of maintaining a child's interest in what they eat is to make mealtimes fun. The sticker chart found at the back of this book is a great way to get kids involved in recording what types of fruits and vegetables they eat each day – and you could take this one step further by charting the colours they eat! There is good reason for this, since it is recommended we try to eat a rainbow of different-coloured fruits and vegetables each day. Variety is the key, since each colour provides a range of healthy phytochemicals (plant nutrients), vitamins and minerals.

Red

Tomatoes, sweet peppers, strawberries, raspberries, watermelon, redcurrants, grapes, cherries, red onions, apples, radishes, rhubarb, red kidney beans, borlotti beans, aduki beans.

These fruits and vegetables (except the beans) are good sources of vitamins C and E, beta-carotene and numerous phytochemicals, including lycopene. The latter is responsible for the natural red colour in tomatoes and has been found to protect us from heart disease and certain cancers. Lycopene becomes more bioavailable when the tomato has been cooked, making a tomato pasta sauce or tomato purée a better source than a raw salad tomato. Iron is found in useful amounts in beans, as is fibre and a number of B vitamins.

Orange

Sweet peppers, carrots, pumpkin, swede, oranges, clementines, tangerines, mandarins, melon, nectarines, peaches, squash, mango, papaya, apricots, guava, lentils.

Providing the orange pigment in citrus fruit are flavanoids. These are antioxidant phytochemicals which help the absorption of vitamin C. Pumpkin and squash contain four times more beta-carotene than a large carrot, which is even more impressive when we consider that a single carrot provides the recommended daily amount. Antioxidants vitamin C and beta-carotene are found in plentiful amounts in all of the above. Lentils are a good source of iron, zinc, folate, manganese, selenium, phosphorus and some B vitamins.

Yellow

Bananas, sweet peppers, courgettes, pineapple, melon, plums, bean sprouts, marrow, sweetcorn, grapefruit, chickpeas, soya beans.

The yellow pigments found in the above fruits and vegetables is due to the presence of plant compounds known as carotenoids. It is believed that these work in tandem with other carotenoids, responsible for red and orange foods, to help protect against cancer and heart disease. Soya beans are a complete protein and are rich in cancer-preventing isoflavones. Bananas help to protect the body from infections and strengthen the digestive system. They also provide plentiful amounts of potassium.

Green

Broccoli, cabbage, Brussels sprouts, sweet peppers, peas, courgettes, apples, pears, kiwi fruit, avocado, spinach, salad leaves, grapes, gooseberries, alfalfa, asparagus, flageolet beans, broad beans.

The carotenoid lutein is present in dark green vegetables. With promising anti-carcinogenic qualities, lutein also helps to prevent age-related blindness. Broccoli is a super-veg, rich in phytochemicals that boost the immune system and protect against cancer. Brussels sprouts and cabbage have similar properties. Kiwi fruit contains more vitamin C than oranges, while apples provide pectin, a soluble fibre that rids the body of unwanted toxins. Avocados offer a perfect balance of carbohydrate, protein and good fats.

Purple

Blueberries, blackcurrants, blackberries, aubergines, figs, beetroot, red cabbage, plums, grapes, black beans.

Like all beans, black beans contain folic acid, which helps to make red blood cells, and are rich in immune-boosting zinc and iron. Rich in phytochemicals, including bioflavanoids, purple fruit and vegetables also contain good amounts of vitamin C. Purple grapes are often given to convalescents, and with good reason, since they contain antiviral and antibacterial properties. They can also improve skin conditions and, like blackberries, have a cleansing effect on the body, helping in the detoxification process.

Quick Fixes

BREAKFAST

We all go through periods of feeling uninspired when it comes to preparing meals for our kids, but with a little planning increasing their fruit and vegetable intake does not have to be difficult. If you are faced with a child who just won't be tempted by a juicy apple or who turns up his or her nose at anything remotely leafy or green, subterfuge may be the only answer! These quick fixes will give you ideas on how to give ready-prepared or popular home-made foods a nutritional boost.

The number of portions given by each serving suggestion equates to the amount of fruit or vegetable a child can fit in his or her hand.

Breakfast is a great time to boost your child's daily quota of fruits and vegetables and wholesome breakfasts need not take a long time to prepare. It's now widely recognized that children who eat a decent breakfast perform better at school. Moreover, research has shown that skipping the first meal of the day can lead to an unhealthy pattern of snacking on high-fat, high-sugar foods mid-morning. The first meal of the day should provide 25 percent of a child's daily nutrient requirement and the following ideas will help you achieve that figure. Why not ditch the high-sugar breakfast cereals and try some of the following instead:

If you have a juicer, use it to make fresh apple and carrot juice or orange and mango.

Alternatively, a glass of fresh fruit juice (not from concentrate or fruit drink) is a simple way to ensure your child is on his or her way to achieving five portions a day.

If serving a cooked breakfast, don't forget the vegetable element: a vegetable-based sausage, grilled tomatoes, sliced mushrooms or baked beans, for example. Each handful of vegetable/bean chosen counts as a single portion.

If your child balks when offered a whole fruit such as an apple, for instance, serving it sliced or chopped can often make it more appealing; try slices of orange, banana, melon, mango, nectarine, apple or peach and arranging them in a pattern on a coloured plate.

Add puréed strawberries and a teaspoon of honey to natural live yogurt.

Fry two chopped spring onions and a quarter of a diced red pepper and stir into scrambled eggs.

Mash a banana into a ready-prepared pancake mix. Top the pancakes with sliced mango and yogurt.

Dip spears of asparagus and sticks of red pepper into a soft-boiled egg.

A stewed apple with a good pinch of cinnamon makes a great topping for a fruit muffin, pancake or waffle.

Add a spoonful of fruit purée to a bowl of warm porridge.

Alternatively, top with a mashed banana.

Stir a chopped grilled tomato or canned plum tomato into a serving of baked beans and serve with whole wheat toast.

Combine finely chopped steamed cabbage with mashed potato and a beaten egg. Form into patties and shallow fry to make potato cakes.

Grated apple is delicious combined with muesli and topped with calcium-rich milk or yogurt.

For a great fruit smoothie, put equal quantities of yogurt and milk in a blender with berries, a banana or peaches and process until creamy.

Ideally, the recommended five portions of fruits and vegetables should be spread throughout the day. It may be difficult to gauge how many of these portions are provided by school lunches, but packed lunches are obviously much easier to monitor.

Add steamed sliced carrot to a home-made or ready-prepared tomato sauce. Blend to make a smooth sauce. Add a handful of chopped mushrooms, sweet peppers, celery, onion or pulses or cooked split red lentils to increase the portion by one.

Top a ready-made pizza base with a home-made tomato sauce and one (or a selection of) the following: a handful of sliced mushrooms, chopped spinach, sliced onion or courgettes, sweetcorn, olives, peas or sweet pepper. Each type of vegetable chosen counts as a single portion.

Sweet pizzas are fun to make. Top a puff pastry base with sliced apple, peach, nectarine or pear. Brush with a little honey or maple syrup and bake at 200ºC for about 25–30 minutes. In summer, try fruit kebabs or make foil parcels containing fruit and put them on the barbecue.

You can't go wrong with fresh fruit salad. Combine chunks of mango, orange and strawberry in a bowl and pour over a small glass of fresh orange juice. Or, for lunch boxes, make your own bags of mixed dried fruit.

Boost the nutrient content of a ready-made vegetable soup by adding some cooked lentils or beans. Purée in a blender if a smooth soup is preferred. Top with a spoonful of home-made humous (see page 121) or some crispy fried onions to further increase the vegetable/bean intake.

Many kids prefer raw vegetables to cooked. Sticks of carrot, celery, red pepper and cucumber are the usual fare, but you could also try mange tout, spring onions, baby corn, sprouted beans, broccoli florets or fennel. Dip into guacamole, humous, bean dip or vegetable purées. Each type of vegetable chosen counts as a single portion.

Canned beans, such as chick peas, cannellini, borlotti or kidney, can form the base of a nutritious salad. Combine with diced, seeded tomato, chopped red pepper and spring onions, and cubes of hard cheese. Drizzle with olive oil and balsamic vinegar or a mixture of mayonnaise and pesto. Each handful of vegetable/bean chosen counts as a single portion.

The evening meal is a good time to ensure your child's eaten his or her daily five. Additionally, certain fruits and vegetables – such as bananas and lettuce – can aid restful sleep (and when a banana is combined with milk, you have the perfect pre-bed combination).

Add favourite vegetables or canned beans to ready-made soups, stews, curries and bakes to boost their nutritional content.

Each type of vegetable/bean chosen counts as a single portion.

Make your own fresh fruit jellies using freshly squeezed juice instead of water and a selection of chopped fruit.

Or, for a quick banana ice cream, wrap a peeled ripe banana in clingfilm and freeze until firm.

Pasta is a perennial favourite and the perfect base for a vegetable sauce. Add chopped spinach to ready-made pesto. Cauliflower, broccoli, leeks or mushrooms can be added to macaroni cheese.

Each handful of vegetable/bean chosen counts as a single portion.

Add cooked grated carrot and onion to mashed potatoes or home-made potato cakes or rosti. (see page 71). Parsnip and celeriac are good alternatives to regular mashed potatoes.

Another great staple is a fresh fruit lolly. Purée a mango, strawberries or peaches with natural live yogurt, then pour into lolly moulds and freeze. Or mix the fruit purée into softened vanilla ice cream.

Alternatively, you can use freshly squeezed fruit juice on its own.

Although baked potatoes don't count as a portion, the toppings can. Try home-made coleslaw (see page 90) combined with grated cheese. Canned or home-made ratatouille, vegetable curry, bean stew, or even the humble canned baked bean are great options.

Combine lean ground beef with grated onion and carrot, herbs, chopped mushrooms and a little beaten egg for a simple home-made burger.

Alternatively, replace the beef with mashed canned beans or cooked lentils to increase the portion of vegetables/beans by one.

Keep it Healthy

It's not just about how much fresh stuff you eat but what you do with it. The way you shop, and how you prepare and cook has a major influence on a fruit or vegetable's nutritional status. For instance, there is a big difference in the nutrient content of a just-picked, organic, locally grown apple that is dispatched to you as part of a box scheme and an apple that has been flown halfway across the world, then displayed for too long on a brightly lit counter. Other things to bear in mind are the length of time the apple is stored once you get it home, as well as whether it is eaten raw or cooked.

Go organic

Organic fresh produce is now widely available and while you may have to pay a little more, the benefits are numerous. Children are believed to be more vulnerable to the effects of

pesticides than adults, for example, and there is good evidence to suggest a connection between pesticide residues and allergies and hyperactivity in children. Another reason for opting for locally grown organic produce is that some "fresh" produce is not actually as fresh as

Buy organic locally

There are many reasons why buying organic food at local organic stores, or farmers' markets is a good idea, but one of the main ones is to get your children involved in appreciating good food. Knowing where their food comes from and just how good it can taste will encourage your children to enjoy "real" food from an early age.

it looks. Apples and carrots, for example, can be stored for up to 12 months in a controlled atmosphere. Potatoes intended for long-term storage may be sprayed with a chemical sprout inhibitor, while citrus fruit are routinely sprayed with a wax preservative.

Organic fruit and vegetables tend to taste better because they are not intensively grown to absorb excessive water and are generally grown in better quality soil. What's more, they are left to ripen longer on the plant, rather than being artificially ripened; a process that can affect both flavour and nutrient levels.

Studies have shown that the lower levels of water in organic produce means there is a higher concentration of vitamins and minerals. However, much of the organic produce we see in the shops comes from abroad. For this reason it is worth checking out the local farmers' markets,

for quality: look for firm, unblemished produce. Treat special offers with suspicion as they may indicate that the retailer has a surplus of produce that is near its sell-by date.

Canned and frozen foods are convenient and often cheaper than fresh, and it is well worth keeping a supply of each as a standby. They can also be more nutritious than some fresh produce, especially if it's been hanging around for a while.

Buy cans without any dents, check the best-before date and look for brands without added sugar and salt. Always buy canned fruit in natural juice rather than syrup.

When buying frozen, check the sell-by date and feel the packet to make sure that the contents – peas for

reputable greengrocers, box schemes or, if feasible, buying direct from farms themselves.

Shopping tips

Fresh, frozen, canned or dried? Fruit and vegetables come in many guises, so the first thing you should decide is which best meets your needs.

Generally, fresh produce should be your first choice but buy as fresh as possible and in small quantities rather than a week's supply, since the longer fruits and vegetables are stored, the less goodness they will contain – nutrients diminish 3–5 days after picking. Buy fresh produce from retailers with a high turnover of goods, and avoid fruits and vegetables displayed in a hot, sunny or over-lit window, as this will influence nutrient levels. Loose fresh produce is much easier to check

Keep it Healthy

instance – are not stuck together in a lump, as this means they may have defrosted and then refrozen, which can result in a loss of vitamin C and may be a danger to health. Make sure that frozen produce is the last to go into your trolley or take a cool bag with you to keep everything frozen until you get home.

Keep it fresh

When you've got your fresh produce home, correct storage is vital to preserve the quality and those precious vitamins and minerals. A vegetable rack kept in a cool, dry place is ideal for most root vegetables; they should keep for 5–6 days, while green vegetables will keep for 3–5 in the fridge. Salad items are best stored in the salad compartment in the bottom of the fridge.

When storing fruit such as apples, pears and oranges, avoid overloading the fruit bowl or they could dry out, bruise or turn mouldy. Bowls of fruit should not be displayed in hot sunlight or in a hot centrally heated room as the contents will ripen and deteriorate quickly. In a warm house, the best place for fruit is in a small bowl kept in a cool place, a vegetable rack stored in a cool, dry place or in the fridge if storing berries and grapes.

Both canned and dried foods are best kept in a dry, cool cupboard. Once opened, dried fruit and pulses should be

transferred to an airtight container. If you display pulses in a glass jar in the kitchen be sure to use and replace them regularly since light can spoil their flavour and reduce their nutrient value.

Get cooking

Fruits and vegetables are generally higher in nutrients when raw rather than cooked, so serve your child some raw produce whenever you can. Try also to avoid peeling fruits and vegetables, as many nutrients are found in or just below the skin. Tear spinach or salad leaves rather than cutting them, as this will reduce the release of enzymes that can destroy nutrients such as vitamin C.

Wash or scrub vegetables but do not soak them, as water-soluble nutrients such as vitamins B and C, will leach into the water.

Cut vegetables into large chunks rather than small pieces, as the less surface area exposed to the air, the more nutrients you'll preserve.

Prepare fruits and vegetables

When cooking is best

Certain nutrients are more readily absorbed when lightly cooked. For instance, lycopene, an antioxidant responsible for the red colour of tomatoes, is more effective after cooking in a sauce or purée. The same goes for beta-carotene, which protects the heart and lungs and is more effective when exposed to heat and oil. However beware of overcooking fruits and vegetables, as nutrients may be lost.

just before cooking or serving, as nutrient levels begin to diminish as soon as the produce is cut. Steaming, stir-frying or microwaving is preferable to boiling. If you do boil vegetables, use the minimum amount of water, then save the cooking water to make stock for soups, gravies and sauces. Never add bicarbonate of soda to preserve the colour of vegetables as this destroys their vitamin C content.

Canned produce simply needs heating through, while frozen fruits and vegetables can be microwaved with a little extra water to help retain nutrients.

How to Eat Five

If you're struggling to get your kids to eat their greens, rest assured you're not alone – even kids who eat plenty of fruits and vegetables have more than likely gone through periods of turning up their nose at anything remotely green. Adults are not off the hook either. While this book is aimed at kids, it's worth remembering that many grown-ups don't eat enough of fruits and vegetables either. So, as a family, make it a mission to start working towards a minimum of five portions a day. Build up gradually, using the chart at the back of this book to monitor the family progress, and make it an enjoyable experience – eating well should not be a penance you have to endure!

Right beginnings

Start as you mean to go on: from six months old, babies can begin to enjoy fruit and vegetable purées mixed with formula or breast milk as a first food. Carrot, parsnip, avocado, banana, pear, apple, mango, melon, pea, leek, peach, cauliflower, broccoli, swede, spinach, squash, pumpkin and courgette all make great purées – and you shouldn't be afraid to experiment with flavours your baby seems to like. Offer a wide range of fruits and vegetables based on what the rest of the family usually eat, since research shows that this might help avoid fussiness later on. Don't forget pulses

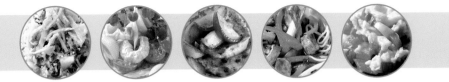

too at this stage, which can be puréed or mashed into stews, soups, bakes or eaten as an accompaniment to a dip. As a baby's iron stores start to diminish after six months, serving pulses with foods rich in vitamin C, such as diluted fresh fruit juice, citrus fruit, broccoli, strawberries, kiwi fruit or spinach, will help to increase iron absorption.

Finger foods

Fruit and vegetable sticks are popular with kids who like their fresh stuff crunchy and tasty. They also make great teethers. When babies start to cut new teeth, finger foods help to relieve sore gums and also give your baby a chance to use his or her hands – far more fun than being fed. Steamed sticks of baby corn, mangetout, green beans and carrot are popular, as are peeled chunks of apple, pear, banana, melon or papaya.

Pre-school children

From around their first birthday, babies begin to show a desire for independence and mealtimes are the perfect time to do this! Toddlers can be very fickle, loving a food one day and disliking it the next. Try to avoid confrontation – coaxing and encouragement are far more rewarding than force-feeding.

Children often make rash decisions, saying that they dislike a meal even before trying it. I've found that if you can encourage them to "try" just one mouthful they often change their minds.

Make it fun

Getting kids involved in shopping, growing, cooking and tasting games are all effective ways of encouraging them to try new or previously rejected fruits and vegetables. Research has shown that children who know where foods come from, who can identify different fruits and vegetables, who have some idea of how they can be used or even have had a go at growing them, are more likely to try and – hopefully – like them.

Depending on the age of your child, adopting a theme for a meal can work well. Something simple such as an "indoor picnic" if the weather is bad can inject a bit of fun into a mealtime. Simply lay a cloth on the floor, choose some brightly coloured plates, cups and cutlery and provide a selection of finger foods.

Try and try again

If your child refuses to try a particular fruit or vegetable, leave it for a few weeks then offer it again in a different guise. Often a rejection is not a true indication of dislike. One

technique, used by a friend of mine who was continually frustrated by the rejection of her culinary creations, was to allow her children to choose five fruits and vegetables they genuinely disliked. She agreed not to give these to her kids on the premise that they would eat everything else. It worked mainly because the children felt empowered and had exercised some choice over what they ate.

Eating together

While it's not always possible for the family to eat together every day, even if you only manage it at weekends, you will begin to reap the rewards. Children learn by example and if they see their parents and other family members enjoying their greens, they may be tempted to try them too. Children can also begin to see mealtimes as an enjoyable family experience, not a chore, a battle ground or the time at which to get up-to-date with the latest TV programme.

Snacking

Young children need snacks. Their tummies are relatively small and cannot cope with large meals, so a couple of small snacks a day will help to keep energy levels up. This is the perfect opportunity to increase the daily quota of fruits and vegetables: sticks of celery filled with cream cheese; a banana sandwich; a handful of dried apricots; humous and oatcakes, for example.

Looking good

Imaginative presentation can make all the difference to the success of a meal. Toddlers who feel they have better things to do than sit down and eat may try a meal that looks fun or resembles a face, boat, house, animal, etc. Most of us don't have the time to do this but, while I feel in the long term it is preferable for kids to appreciate "real" food, now and again this can be a useful

has a healthy appetite round to your house to play can have far more effect on your own children than years of coaxing and persuasion.

Experiment

With such a wide range of fruits and vegetables to choose from, it's unlikely that your child will dislike them all. Don't get stuck in a rut, try buying a different fruit or vegetable each week, or experiment with preparation. Cook them in a variety of ways – raw, griddled, roasted, baked, steamed, mashed or stir-fried. It can be as simple as cutting fruits and vegetables into different shapes or adding extra fresh produce to classic children's favourites such as pizza and burgers. If all else fails, subterfuge may be the only answer!

technique. One very simple idea is to use different coloured or shaped foods and arrange them in an attractive way – in a pattern on a colourful plate, for example. Or keep a colourful bowl of fruit out on display, letting kids help themselves, but remember not to overload the bowl to keep the fruit fresh and to change the selection regularly.

School children

When children start school, you have the added challenge of overcoming peer pressure. It only took a friend of my daughter's to announce that she hated peas for my daughter to stop eating them with immediate effect – and for quite some time. This may sound a little manipulative, but inviting a child who you know

FRUITS

An Apple a Day …

The ultimate convenience food, apples need little embellishment and come in a huge number of varieties, each with its own special flavour. Smaller apples are easier for children to eat (and usually sweeter). If your little one turns his or her nose up when offered an apple, coring and slicing it can make it more appealing, but apples begin to lose their vitamins as soon as they are cut, so serve cut fruit immediately.

ONE PORTION
1 small to medium apple

An excellent source of energy, phytochemicals and antioxidants, especially vitamin C, apples also provide valuable fibre in the form of pectin. The natural food pigments or anthocyanins found in apples are said to have anti-carcinogenic properties and may also reduce cholesterol and prevent blood clots. In natural medicine, the blood purifying qualities of apples are highly valued, as is their ability to aid digestion and remove impurities from the liver.

Maximize the nutrients

Always choose organic if possible. Most of the pesticides used on non-organic apples collect in the core and seeds, so remove these if you are cooking the fruit. Since the nutrients are concentrated in and just below the skin, it is best to avoid peeling apples, the skins also provide valuable soluble fibre. Apples continue to ripen after they are picked and are best when in season.

Home-grown apples bought out of season may have spent several months in cold storage, where ripening is artificially halted. When they are taken out of storage they begin to deteriorate quickly and turn soft. Look for undamaged fruit with no bruises and squeeze gently before buying to ensure the apple is firm, but don't be seduced by apples that look too perfect, they are often woolly textured.

HOW TO EAT MORE...
- *Preheat the grill to medium and line the grill pan with foil. Halve an apple lengthways, scoop out the core and arrange on the grill pan. Put slices of Cheddar or mozzarella cheese on top of each apple half then grill until the apple has softened and the cheese has melted and begins to turn golden.*
- *Add grated apple — there's no need to peel it first — to sandwich fillings, coleslaw, breakfast cereals and home-made burgers.*

TOFFEE APPLE CINNAMON BUNS

Revive your child's interest in breakfast with this simple fruity recipe that will help enliven body and mind for the morning ahead.

SERVES 4

- 3–4 apples (scrubbed if not organic), halved and cored
- 1 tsp lemon juice
- 55 g/2 oz unsalted butter
- 2 tbsp maple syrup
- 4 currant buns, halved
- 2 free-range eggs, beaten
- 4 tbsp milk
- cinnamon, for sprinkling

1 Thinly slice each apple half, then toss in lemon juice to prevent them from going brown.

2 Melt three-quarters of the butter in a heavy-based frying pan, then add the apple slices and cook over a medium heat for about 2 minutes until they begin to soften. Pour in the maple syrup and cook for a further 1–2 minutes until the apple slices are tender.

3 Transfer the apples and sauce to a bowl and keep warm while you prepare the cinnamon buns.

4 Mix together the eggs and milk in a shallow bowl. Wipe the frying pan and melt the remaining butter. Dip each half of the currant buns into the egg mixture and place in the hot pan – you will have to cook the buns in two batches – and cook each side until lightly golden. You may have to add more butter when you are cooking the second batch of buns.

5 Arrange two halves of fruit bun on each serving plate. Pile the apple slices on top of each bun and spoon over a little of the syrup. Sprinkle with cinnamon before serving.

Going Bananas

When your child is feeling anxious or having difficulty sleeping, try giving him or her a banana and a glass of milk a couple of hours before bedtime. Bananas and milk contain both the calm-inducing vitamin B_6 and tryptophan, an amino acid that stimulates the production of the neurotransmitter serotonin, which in turn has a calming, relaxing and uplifting effect on the body and mind – quite an asset when it comes to children! Alternatively, if your child is anti-breakfast, a banana may go down well, especially if topped with natural yogurt and a swirl of maple syrup and toasted chopped nuts and seeds for a crunchy topping. Bananas are full of beneficial nutrients and are great for growing children. Their high starch or natural sugar content makes them a good source of sustained energy, particularly if combined with a protein food such as nuts or seeds. In natural medicine, bananas

ONE PORTION
1 small banana

are said to strengthen the stomach and are an effective laxative. Initial studies show that the natural sugars found in bananas also encourage the growth of beneficial bacteria in the intestines, helping to improve nutrient absorption. Bananas also contain significant amounts of potassium, important for cell function, nerves and muscles, and useful amounts of iron, calcium, beta-carotene and vitamin C.

Maximize the nutrients

The nutrients found in bananas are most readily absorbed when the fruit is ripe, shown by a uniformly yellow skin. Under-ripe bananas are difficult to digest and can cause painful wind. When the fruit turns completely brown or black it is too ripe to eat but can still be used in cooking. Don't store bananas in the fridge as the skins will blacken, and bear in mind that bananas kept in a fruit bowl will hasten the ripening of other fruit. When cooked, bananas lose much of their vitamin B_6 content but the fibre content is more readily usable.

BANANA PANCAKES WITH SUMMER BERRY SAUCE

These pancakes can also be served plain or flavoured with blueberries or apple purée.

SERVES 4

- 175 g/6 oz plain flour
- 1 tsp baking powder
- large pinch of salt
- 25 g/1 oz unrefined caster sugar
- 1 egg, beaten
- 200 ml/7 fl oz milk
- 1 large banana, mashed
- 25 g/1 oz unsalted butter
- natural bio yogurt, to serve

Summer berry sauce:
- 250 g/8 oz frozen summer berries, defrosted
- 1–2 tbsp icing sugar

1 For the sauce: purée the berries until smooth. Press the mixture through a sieve, then stir in the icing sugar.

2 For the batter: sieve the flour, baking powder and salt into a mixing bowl then stir in the sugar. Whisk together the egg and milk and gradually add to the mixture, stirring with a wooden spoon. Leave to stand for 30 minutes, then stir in the banana.

1-2

3 Melt half the butter in a large heavy-based frying pan over a medium heat. Ladle three tbsp of batter per pancake into the frying pan and cook each side for about 2 minutes. Repeat with the rest of the batter.

4 Serve two pancakes per person with the berry sauce and yogurt.

HOW TO EAT MORE...

- *Curb the spiciness of curries by adding a sliced banana.*
- *Split a banana lengthways – but not all the way through. Press a few pieces of chopped chocolate into the split, then wrap the banana tightly in foil. Bake in a preheated oven, 200°C/400°F, for 20–25 minutes until the banana skin is blackened and the chocolate melted. Carefully open the foil parcel and sprinkle with chopped nuts.*
- *Bananas go well with strawberries, peaches, nectarines, blueberries, mango, apricots and raspberries. Add coconut milk, yogurt, ice cream or milk as well as a sprinkling of nutmeg or cinnamon to make a tasty, creamy smoothie.*

Clever Citrus

Many of us are put off oranges because they can be hard for a child to peel, yet mandarins and their hybrid tangerines, satsumas and clementines win hands down on this count. Called "easy-peelers" for this reason, they make a useful and healthy addition to lunch boxes and picnics. Clementines are the favoured citrus fruit in my house, as the segments are usually sweet and there are no pips. Satsumas can sometimes be disappointing, the flesh woolly and lacking in flavour. Mandarins are most commonly sold canned and are great for decorating cheesecakes, trifles or sundaes, or in fruit jellies.

Navel oranges are very popular – they contain no pips and are good for slicing. Look also for Jaffa and Valencia oranges, which are sweet and great for juicing. Both oranges and clementines can be used in much the same way and are very versatile. The juice gives a zesty flavour when added to marinades or used to make a sweet glaze for vegetables, fish and meat.

Citrus fruits are particularly rich in the immune-boosting vitamin C and beta-carotene. The jury is still out on whether vitamin C actually prevents colds, but researchers certainly agree that it can lessen the severity and length of the common cold. It also boosts the body's ability to absorb iron from food, which is particularly valuable as iron deficiency is one of the most common nutritional problems in children. Along with an abundance of vitamin C and the B vitamins, thiamine and folate, citrus fruits provide phytochemicals, plant compounds that help in fighting many common health problems, including allergies, asthma and cancer. Citrus fruits also contain pectin, a type of soluble fibre that is said to help reduce cholesterol levels.

ONE PORTION
1–2 clementines, tangerines or satsumas

Maximize the nutrients

Citrus fruits start to lose their vitamin C content as soon as they are cut. Vitamin C is also reduced by heat and is water-soluble, so eat citrus fruit as soon as it's peeled to retain as many nutrients as possible. Freshly squeezed juice retains much of its vitamin C content and squeezing juice at home is preferable to shop-bought juices, but drink as soon after juicing as possible. Concentrated fruit juices go through an additional production process that diminishes the nutrient content, so they are best avoided if possible.

Choose fruits that are heavy for their size – thin-skinned fruit tend to be the juiciest. It's easier to check for quality and often cheaper to buy loose

KID PLEASING
Wonderfully versatile, oranges and tangerines make great drinks and add zest to biscuits and cakes. Dip segments in melted chocolate for a treat!

▼

HOW TO EAT MORE...

- *Mix orange juice with soy sauce, honey, ginger and garlic and use as a marinade for chicken, salmon, meat or tofu.*
- *Sliced, peeled orange and tangerine segments are great in salads containing watercress or Cos lettuce, beetroot and chopped walnuts.*
- *Melt some butter with orange juice in a saucepan and use as a glaze for lightly steamed carrots, cabbage, Brussels sprouts or baby turnips.*
- *Add orange juice to a tomato sauce to give extra zing or use orange juice to lubricate a stir-fry or fresh fruit salad.*
- *Stir lemon juice and honey into warm water for a soothing drink.*
- *Combine orange and lemon juice with sparkling mineral water or soda water for a quick, healthy alternative to high-sugar fizzy drinks. Juice oranges with carrots and apples for an energizing start to the day.*

fruits rather than pre-packed. Oranges tend to keep well, more so than tangerines and other "easy-peelers". When a recipe calls for orange zest, use unwaxed fruit or scrub thoroughly to get rid of the wax, which acts as a preservative. This will also remove any fungicides that may have been used.

PEEK-A-BOO CITRUS JELLIES

Children love these pretty orange shells filled with a sherbet orange and lemon jelly. The oranges take a little time to scoop out, but they're worth the effort. For simplicity, I've used a combination of fresh fruit juice and real fruit lemon jelly crystals to make the filling. You can buy jelly crystals in health food shops and some supermarkets. If preferred, you can use tangerines instead of oranges but slice off the top rather than cut the fruit in half.

SERVES 4

- 4 oranges, halved crossways
- 1 packet real fruit lemon jelly crystals

1 Juice the orange halves without breaking or squashing the skin – a reamer or citrus squeezer are good for this. Using a melon baller or teaspoon, scrape out the pith from the orange halves to leave 8 hollowed-out shells. Strain the juice into a jug – then drink half of it!

2 Add the jelly crystals to the jug containing the remaining orange juice and top up with boiling water to make 568 ml/ 1 pint. Stir well until the crystals have dissolved.

3 Place the orange shells on a baking tray. Fill each shell with the liquid jelly and chill until set.

4 To serve, place two halves on top of one another to hide the jelly inside – you could even tie a ribbon around the outside for a decorative party effect.

CHOCOLATE ORANGE MOUSSE

This mousse is rich so this isn't an everyday dessert – but it is a very special treat. This dessert contains uncooked eggs.

SERVES 4

- 200 g/7 oz good quality plain chocolate, broken into small chunks
- juice of 2 oranges
- 4 free-range eggs, separated
- 4 clementines or satsumas, peeled and segmented

1 Melt the chocolate in a heat-proof bowl placed over a pan of gently simmering water. Make sure the bottom of the bowl does not touch the water. Stir the chocolate until melted.

2 Leave the chocolate to cool, then stir in the orange juice and egg yolks.

ORANGE & MANGO SHERBET

3 Whisk the egg whites in a large bowl until they form stiff peaks. Using a metal spoon, gently fold the egg whites into the chocolate mixture one spoonful at a time.

4 Spoon the mousse into bowls or ramekins and chill until set. Decorate with segments of clementine or satsuma.

Super fruity and easy to make, this vibrant ice is a favourite with kids. The combination of orange juice and mango is refreshing and is a great source of vitamin C and beta-carotene.

SERVES 4

- 2 mangoes
- 300 ml/½ pint fresh orange juice
- 3 tbsp caster sugar

1 Cut the mangoes either side of the large central stone and slice off any flesh around the stone. Scoop out the flesh from the mango slices and place in a blender or food processor. Add the orange juice and sugar to the blender and process until puréed and smooth.

2 Pour the mixture into a freezer-proof container and freeze for 2 hours. Remove from the freezer and beat with a whisk or fork to break up the ice crystals, smooth the top with the back of a spoon and return to the freezer. Repeat this process after another 2 hours, then freeze until solid.

3 Remove from the freezer 45 minutes before serving to allow the ice to soften.

1-2

Appetizing Apricots

Their golden-orange colour indicates that apricots are an excellent source of the antioxidant beta-carotene. In fact, the brighter and juicier the fruit, the more beta-carotene it contains. Beta-carotene has been shown to help prevent many degenerative diseases, including cancer. It is also believed to combat free radical damage and help boost the immune system.

ONE PORTION
1–2 fresh apricots, depending on child's age

Apricots are one of the few fruits that I buy canned. While there is nothing more luscious than a ripe juicy fresh apricot, finding them at their best is often difficult. When they are unripe, apricots are hard and tasteless, and unfortunately they do not continue to ripen after picking. Canned apricots in syrup have a high sugar content so opt instead for fruit in natural juice, which is also a useful source of vitamin C.

Dried apricots (see pages 64–5) are another option and a good source of iron.

Maximize the nutrients

When buying fresh apricots, try to buy them ripe and eat them within a couple of days of purchase as they don't keep well. Try not to buy very under-ripe fruit as they rarely reach their best (however, don't give up, as these less-than-perfect fruits can be stewed, poached or used in cakes and tarts). Apricots are delicate and can be easily bruised, so care is needed when buying and storing. Look for undamaged fruit and store them at room temperature or in a polythene bag in the fridge.

Research has found that although cooked apricots have reduced levels of vitamin C, nutrients such as beta-carotene and lycopene are actually made more readily available to the body when the fruit is cooked.

HOW TO EAT MORE...

- *Add chopped apricots to pilaffs, couscous, curries and vegetable or bean stews.*
- *Try apricot sauce with pork or other meat. Put 5 chopped apricots in a pan with a little water, 1 clove and a cinnamon stick. Cook for about 8 minutes, remove the spices and purée or mash roughly with a fork. Add a little sugar to taste.*
- *Spice up porridge with a large spoonful of apricot purée (above) or swirl into yogurt or fromage frais. Add some toasted nuts and oats and you have a nutritious breakfast.*

APRICOT BRIOCHE BUTTER PUDDING

Brioche adds a richness to this bread and butter pudding but you could also use panettone, fruit bread, hot cross buns or good old sliced white or wholemeal bread. I used canned apricots in natural juice when I tested this recipe as fresh were unavailable. However, in this case canned is no compromise. Alternatively, you could try dried apricots. To increase the fruit content you could also add a handful of raisins or dried chopped dates.

SERVES 6

- butter, for spreading
- 280 g/10 oz brioche, cut into 10 slices, then triangles
- 20 canned apricot halves in natural juice, drained and roughly chopped.
- 2 free-range egg yolks
- 4 tbsp maple syrup
- 1 tsp vanilla essence
- 500 ml/18 fl oz milk
- grated nutmeg, to taste
- demerara sugar, optional

1 Preheat the oven to 180°C/ 350°F. Butter a 22 x 30 cm ovenproof dish, then lightly butter one side of each triangle of brioche.

2 Arrange half the brioche in the dish, top with apricots, and put the remaining brioche on top.

3 Mix together the egg yolks, maple syrup and vanilla essence. Warm the milk, then whisk into the egg mixture. Add grated nutmeg to taste.

4 Pour the egg mixture over the brioche, and lightly press down. Sprinkle with the demerara sugar, if using, and bake for 25 minutes until risen and golden.

Take a Pear …

For many children, pears are their first "real" food and consequently evoke fond memories. Pears are one of the least allergenic of foods, which is why they are appropriate as a weaning food and can be tolerated by those on exclusion diets or children prone to food allergies. Pears are high in natural sugars, so provide a convenient and useful source of energy. Vitamin C and potassium are also found in beneficial amounts.

Most pears are suitable for eating raw or cooked, but they should be peeled if you are cooking them. The green- and brown-skinned Conference; plump greeny-yellow Comice; and Williams with its thin, yellow skin and sweet, soft flesh, are particular favourites with many children.

Dried pears make a convenient snack and provide a good source of iron, but remember that the sugar content is concentrated during the drying process so dried pears can be very sweet.

ONE PORTION
1 small to medium pear

Like other orchard fruits, pears are great with sweet and savoury dishes, either as a puréed fruit sauce with meat, chopped in to crunchy winter salads, or cooked in compotes, tarts, pies or crumbles. They can be grilled, sautéed or poached. When cooking pears use slightly under-ripe fruit as they are prone to disintegrate if too ripe. In fact over-ripe pears are pretty unpleasant as they become woolly textured and mushy.

Maximize the nutrients

If you are going to eat the pears within a day or so of buying them, choose fully ripened fruit and keep them in the fridge. They will be past their best and lose nutrients if you want to keep them for any longer than this. I tend to buy pears slightly under-ripe (or ideally a mixture of ripe and slightly under-ripe), so that they will last a few days in the fruit bowl. To tell if a pear is ripe, feel around the base of the stalk – where it should give slightly when gently pressed – but the pear itself should be firm.

Uncooked ripe pears are richer in vitamin C than cooked, although the fibre count will be lower if they are peeled. Pears discolour quickly when peeled, so sprinkle the cut surface with a little lemon juice.

PEAR & PLUM CRUMBLE

Comforting and warming, crumbles are perfect for using up fruit that is not as its peak or is slightly under-ripe.

SERVES 4

- 4 slightly under-ripe pears, peeled, cored and roughly chopped
- 6 plums, stoned and roughly chopped
- 1 tsp lemon juice
- 4 tbsp fresh apple juice
- ¼ tsp mixed spice
- 1 tbsp soft brown sugar

For the topping:
- 115 g/4 oz unsalted butter
- 175 g/6 oz plain flour
- 3 tbsp sunflower seeds
- 85 g/3 oz soft brown sugar

1 Preheat the oven to 180°C/ 350°F. Combine the pears, plums, lemon juice, apple juice, mixed spice and sugar in a 25 cm/10 in ovenproof dish.

2 To make the topping, use your fingers to mix the butter into the flour until the texture resembles coarse breadcrumbs. Carefully stir in the seeds and sugar.

3 Spoon the topping onto the fruit and bake in the oven for about 30 minutes until the crumble is golden and crisp. Leave to cool slightly before serving.

HOW TO EAT MORE...

- *Pears make a great addition to salads and go well with rocket, watercress, finely grated white cabbage, celery, cheese and nuts.*
- *Halve a ripe pear and scoop out the core. Fill the cavity with soft cream cheese.*
- *Baked pears look pretty and are easy to prepare. Simply peel, cut in half and scoop out the core of a slightly under-ripe pear. Brush each pear half with lemon juice and place in an ovenproof dish. Pour orange juice into the dish and drizzle with a little honey. Bake the pears in an oven preheated to 180°C/350°F for 20–30 minutes until softened and sticky, spooning over the juices occasionally.*
- *Alternatively, peel and core a pear and fill the cavity with a mixture of dried fruits and chopped nuts. Put the whole pear in an ovenproof dish with a little water and honey and bake as above.*

Strawberry Fair

There's nothing nicer than a ripe, juicy strawberry. In the past a sign of summer, strawberries are now available all year, but try to buy them in season for the best, most nutritious fruit.

A very good source of vitamin C, strawberries help boost the immune system and protect connective tissues. Research has also found that they contain a collection of powerful plant pigments called anthocyanins. These antioxidants protect against harmful toxins and free radicals in the body as well as protecting precious brain cells. Strawberries also contain ellagic acid, which plays an important role in defeating and preventing cancer.

Maximize the nutrients

Kids are more vulnerable to the effects of pesticides and antibiotics than adults, so it's wise to opt for organic strawberries whenever possible. Always choose ripe strawberries and avoid those that have white or yellow tips, as this is a sign that they are under-ripe. Conversely, avoid mushy and bruised fruits as these are past their best and will have lost many of their beneficial nutrients. You can store them in the refrigerator for up to 3 days, and they are also suitable for freezing.

Cooking does not appear to destroy the ellagic acid in strawberries but it will deplete levels of folates and vitamin C.

KID PLEASING
Most kids love strawberries and readily eat them straight. But if your child dislikes the pips, serving them in a pudding will go down a treat.

QUEEN OF HEARTS PUDDING

ONE PORTION
A handful or 5 depending on your child's age

You can sieve the berries to remove any pips, but leave the fruit whole if this is not a problem with your children. Use a pastry cutter to cut the bread into heart shapes.

SERVES 4

- 450 g/1 lb strawberries, raspberries and blackberries, hulled and the large fruit sliced
- 4–5 tbsp caster sugar
- 6 tbsp water
- 8 slices day-old white bread, crusts removed

1 Put the berries in a saucepan with the sugar and water. Bring to the boil, then simmer for 5 minutes or until the fruit is soft and juicy. Reserve a few whole berries then press the rest of the fruit through a sieve, extracting as much juice as possible.

2 With a pastry cutter, cut the bread slices into heart shapes.

3 Place half the bread shapes in a shallow dish and spoon over half the fruit juice. Top with the remaining bread and spoon over the rest of the juice. Press down lightly so the juice soaks right into the bread and leave for about 30 minutes. Decorate the top with the reserved berries, and serve.

HOW TO EAT MORE...

- *Sprinkle a handful of hulled and sliced strawberries on top of breakfast cereal. Their vitamin C will boost the absorption of iron from the cereal.*
- *Make a strawberry sauce to use hot or cold over ice cream or pancakes. Purée a handful of strawberries in a blender. Add a little caster sugar to taste. Strain to remove any pips.*
- *Make a fruit smoothie using a handful of strawberries, live yogurt and a teaspoon of honey, if you need to add sweetness. (To triple the portion count, combine with an orange and a banana.)*
- *Whip up some yogurt ice cream. Follow the instructions above for the smoothie but quadruple the amount of fruit and yogurt, then freeze. Whisk 3–4 times during the freezing process to give a creamy, smooth texture.*

Bountiful Berries

These small baubles of goodness contain an abundance of nutrients, especially vitamin C, valued for boosting the immune system and improving the condition of the skin, bones and teeth.

Blueberries are one of the few berries that are sweet enough never to require a sprinkling of sugar – just a handful makes a highly nutritious snack. Studies suggest that blueberries help to enhance memory, may improve motor skills and play a vital role in preventing cancer and heart disease. Their anti-bacterial properties may help fight tummy upsets too.

Like blueberries, raspberries and blackberries are good sources of vitamin C and folate as well as the antioxidants ellagic acid and quercetin, which are also thought to be anti-carcinogenic. They are said to help prevent cold sores, hay fever and asthma, all prevalent among children.

In natural medicine raspberries are said to cleanse and soothe the system and act as a cooling remedy for fever.

ONE PORTION
A handful of berries

KID PLEASING
Blueberries are naturally sweet and have soft seeds – both bonus points when it comes to children.

Maximize the nutrients

You can buy most berries all year round, but they are at their best when in season during the summer and early autumn. Berries freeze well and frozen berries are said to be as healthy as fresh, in fact they may even retain nutrients for longer. Cooking does not seem to destroy the beneficial anti-carcinogen ellagic acid found in berries, but it will diminish the levels of folate and vitamin C.

When canned, berries lose many of their nutritional benefits and are high in sugar if packed in syrup.

APPLE, BERRY & CUSTARD TURNOVERS

Blueberries or blackberries (or a mixture of different berries) are delicious in these pastries. The turnovers go down well in lunchboxes.

1-2

MAKES ABOUT 8-10

- 2 dessert apples, unpeeled, cored and cut into small dice
- 150 g/5½ oz blackberries or blueberries
- ½ tsp lemon juice
- 1 tbsp unrefined caster sugar, plus extra for sprinkling
- 500 g/1 lb 2 oz ready-made puff pastry
- flour, for dusting
- 1 free-range egg, beaten
- 10 heaped tsp ready-made custard

1 Preheat the oven to 200°C/ 400°F. Mix together the apples, berries and lemon juice in a bowl. Stir in the sugar.

2 Roll out the pastry on a lightly floured surface until about 2 mm/¹⁄₁₆ in thick. Cut out 8 15 cm/6 in circles. Moisten the edge of each pastry circle with a little of the beaten egg.

3 Place two tbsp of fruit in the centre of each circle and top with a heaped tsp of custard.

4 Fold the pastry over the filling to make a half-moon shape. Pinch together the pastry edges to seal. Place the turnovers on a lightly greased baking sheet and brush the tops with egg. Prick each one with a fork and sprinkle with a little extra sugar. Bake for about 20 minutes until risen and golden.

HOW TO EAT MORE...

- *Make your own fruit yogurt: simply purée a handful of berries, sieve to remove any seeds, then stir into natural bio yogurt. Add a little honey to sweeten and add toasted oats, seeds or chopped nuts.*
- *Puréed berries, sweetened with icing sugar, can be added to fizzy mineral water to make a delicious fruity drink.*
- *Berries make great smoothies and go well with bananas, peaches, mango, nectarines and cherries. Add natural bio yogurt and a handful of muesli or crunchy cereal to make a tasty breakfast treat.*
- *For the classic summer dessert Eton Mess, lightly whip a carton of whipping cream and mix in a splash of vanilla extract and caster sugar to sweeten. Stir in some crumbled meringues and a handful of raspberries.*

Cheery Cherries

Cherries vary in colour from golden yellow to deep red and almost black. They vary in sweetness too, ranging from sour (suitable for cooking) to sweet (best for eating "raw"), with a few varieties that fit into both camps. Sweet cherries are not great when cooked as they tend to lose some of their flavour, so if using in a compote, pie or tart, opt for a slightly sour and more acidic variety such as Montmorency.

Uncooked sweet cherries are a good source of vitamin C and potassium, which is essential for normal water balance and blood pressure. Cherries also contain many phytochemicals, known for their health-giving properties (see page 8) and there is some evidence that cherry juice can reduce the incidence of tooth decay and help reduce the pain of inflammation and headaches. Rutin is also found in significant amounts in cherries, which may enhance the efficacy of vitamin C and maintain healthy veins and capillaries. In natural medicine, cherries are believed to stimulate and cleanse the whole body, removing toxins from the kidneys.

PORTION SIZE
1 handful of cherries.

Maximize the nutrients

When looking for cherries, go for ripe, bright, glossy-skinned fruit without any blemishes and a green stalk, an indication of freshness and optimum nutrient content. Although cherries are now available all year round, as with most fruits, they tend to be at their very best when in season. Those available out of season are likely to have travelled a long way to reach the shops. Frozen cherries are an excellent convenient alternative to fresh and retain much of their vitamin C content.

A great deal of the vitamin C in cherries is lost when they are cooked, so eat cherries uncooked when possible. Store them in the fridge too, to reduce vitamin C deterioration, and only wash just before serving.

Initial research shows that certain substances found in cherries may reduce the level of potentially carcinogenic compounds that form in meat and fish when they are cooked.

CHOCOLATE CHERRY SUNDAE

A "Black Forest gateau in a glass", without the alcohol, of course. Chocolate, cherries and whipped cream are a wonderful combination.

SERVES 4

- 400 g/14 oz can cherries in syrup
- 280 g/10 oz ripe cherries with stalks
- 200 ml/7 fl oz double or whipping cream
- 4 chocolate muffins, halved

1 Drain the canned cherries into a bowl, reserving 4 tbsp of the syrup. Purée the cherries in a blender until smooth, then stir in the reserved syrup.

2 Remove the stalks, halve and pit the fresh cherries, reserving four (with stalks if possible). You can chop the fresh cherries further if desired. Whip the cream until it forms soft peaks.

3 Take four tall sundae glasses and place half a chocolate muffin in each. Spoon over the cherry purée and divide half the fresh cherries between the glasses. Top with the whipped cream. Repeat the layers until the glasses are full, finishing with cream.

4 Decorate each sundae with a whole fresh cherry.

HOW TO EAT MORE...

- *Clafoutis is a traditional French dessert made with a sweetened batter mix containing cherries. It is baked in an ovenproof dish until golden and risen. You can also make it with strawberries, pears or apples.*
- *Dip cherries into melted chocolate for a sweet treat. If the stalk is intact this makes dipping that much easier.*
- *For children who dislike raisins, dried cherries may be an acceptable alternative. Use in cakes, scones, cookies and muffins.*
- *Cherries are delicious poached to make a compote or fruit jelly.*
- *Combine pitted cherries with peach juice and a banana in a blender to make a fruity drink. Cherries are also good with blackberries, blueberries, strawberries or mango.*
- *Sprinkle a handful of sweet pitted cherries over breakfast cereal.*

Pineapple Perfection

It is the astonishing appearance of fresh pineapple that makes it so appealing to kids. Its fragrant flavour lends itself to both sweet and savoury dishes. Traditionally served with ham and gammon and with cheese, pineapple also goes well with fish and poultry and is often used in Chinese cooking in sweet and sour dishes. Children seem to love the combination of sweet and sour flavours, and they make a perfect foil for vegetables such as carrots, sweetcorn, cabbage, green beans, sweet peppers, mushrooms and aubergines.

Rich in vitamin C, fresh pineapple is also reputed to relieve constipation, catarrh, arthritis and urinary tract infections as well as settling upset stomachs. It also contains an enzyme called bromelain, which is an anti-inflammatory. In terms of nutritional content and flavour, fresh pineapple is preferable to canned, although the latter makes a convenient store cupboard standby.

ONE PORTION
A small to medium slice

Maximize the nutrients

When buying a pineapple, choose one that has a strong sweet smell and fresh green leaves. To test for ripeness try pulling out a leaf at its base – if it comes out easily the fruit is ripe. Pineapples do not become any sweeter after picking so don't buy an unripe fruit as you'll be disappointed with its flavour. Fresh pineapple is marginally richer in vitamin C than canned, but the canning process destroys the bromelain content. Cooking reduces the vitamin C content but makes the soluble fibre content more readily available.

HOW TO EAT MORE...

- *Wrap a slice of bacon around a long slice of fresh pineapple then grill until the bacon is beginning to crisp.*
- *Use pineapple juice in place of vinegar to make a delicious fruity salad dressing or marinade base.*
- *For a refreshing granita, chop 300 g/10½ oz cored pineapple in a food processor. Stir in 1 tsp grated fresh root ginger. Spoon into a freezer-proof container and freeze for about 2½ hours. Stir to break up the ice crystals and serve. Add chunks of mango to increase the fruit count.*

SWEET & SOUR EGGY RICE

Although I'm not a fan of overly sugary sweet-and-sour sauces, this recipe successfully adopts the principle of combining a sweet food with a savoury one. You could add three beaten eggs to the stir-fried vegetables before adding the rice to make egg fried rice, but I prefer to make an omelette and serve it in strips on the top of the rice.

SERVES 4

- 1 tbsp sunflower oil
- 1 large onion, roughly chopped
- 2 cloves garlic, finely chopped
- 1–2 tsp grated fresh root ginger
- 2 pak choi, very finely chopped
- 85 g/3 oz frozen peas
- 85 g/3 oz diced fresh pineapple with 4 tbsp juice, or canned pineapple in natural juice
- 550 g/1 lb 4 oz cooked brown rice, left to cool

- 2 tsp dark soy sauce
- 2 tsp butter
- 6 free-range eggs, beaten

1 Heat the oil in a large wok or heavy-based frying pan. Stir-fry the onion for 5 minutes until tender, then add the garlic, ginger, pak choi and peas then stir-fry for another 3 minutes.

2 Add the pineapple and juice then stir in the rice and soy sauce. Toss the rice until heated through; keep warm while you cook the omelettes.

3 Heat half the butter in a frying pan and add half the egg. Swirl it around until it coats the bottom of the pan. Cook until the egg sets, then turn out onto a plate and cut into strips. Repeat with the remaining egg.

4 Serve the pineapple rice topped with the strips of omelette.

Grape News!

Nature's healers, grapes are traditionally given to us when we feel unwell and there's a good reason for this: grapes provide iron, potassium and fibre, and in natural medicine they are known for their detoxifying and cleansing properties. Furthermore, grapes contain phytochemicals that may help to reduce the risk of cancer and heart disease.

Grapes come in various shades, but red/purple grapes have the highest concentration of nutrients. The key natural substance in grapes is a compound called resveratrol. It is found in the skin of red grapes and has anticarcinogenic properties.

For children, the appeal of grapes is their size and sweetness. Seedless grapes are preferred for obvious reasons, however they are also lower in tannin, an effective antioxidant that works as an antibiotic, soaking up the bacteria that causes tooth decay.

ONE PORTION
A child's handful
of grapes

Maximize the nutrients

The best way to tell if grapes are at their best is to taste one. A perfect bunch of grapes should have plump fruit of equal size – tiny grapes will taste sour. Avoid any grapes with signs of bruising, mould or wrinkled skin. Over-ripe grapes will fall off the branch and be past their best.

Unless they are organic, grapes should be thoroughly washed before eating as they are routinely sprayed with pesticides and fungicides. Unwashed fruit can be stored in a polythene bag in the fridge for about a week.

KID PLEASING
If your child refuses to eat grapes, try grape juice, it's delicious and retains many of the disease-fighting compounds of the grape.

FRUIT & NUT NUGGETS

Your child can take part in making this crunchy breakfast cereal. It is a nutritious meld of honey-coated oats, nuts, seeds and fruit. As an alternative to the yogurt, you could serve this cereal with milk and scatter over a handful of grapes.

3

SERVES 10

- 55 g/2 oz Brazil nuts
- 55 g/2 oz whole hazelnuts
- 140 g/5 oz whole porridge oats
- 55 g/2 oz sunflower seeds
- 40 g/1½ oz pumpkin seeds
- 2 tbsp sunflower oil
- 4 tbsp runny honey
- 85 g/3 oz raisins
- 85 g/3 oz ready-to-eat unsulphured dried apricots, roughly chopped
- natural bio yogurt and seedless red grapes, halved, to serve

1 Preheat the oven to 140°/275°F. Roughly chop the Brazil nuts and hazelnuts in a food processor, or place them in a plastic bag and hit them with the end of a rolling pin until roughly broken. Put the chopped nuts in a mixing bowl with the oats and seeds.

2 Gently heat the oil and honey in a saucepan. Stir until the honey has melted, then stir into the oats mixture until the contents of the bowl are coated.

3 Spread the mixture in an even layer onto two baking sheets and cook in the oven for 35 minutes, stirring occasionally, until slightly golden and crisp – the mixture will become more crisp as it cools.

4 Transfer the cereal to a large mixing bowl and stir in the raisins and apricots. Leave to cool then store in an airtight jar.

5 To serve, sprinkle a handful of the cereal into a tall glass and top with a layer of yogurt. Arrange some halved seeded grapes over the yogurt and repeat the layers, finishing with a layer of grapes.

HOW TO EAT MORE...

- *Finely chop a handful of seedless grapes and combine with grated Cheddar cheese or slices of Brie to make a delicious sandwich filling.*
- *Cook dried raisins and apricots in red grape juice until tender, then purée to make a fruit spread.*
- *For mini pavlovas, halve a handful of seeded grapes and combine with cubes of melon, mango or nectarines. Pour over a little orange juice and use as a topping for individual meringues, filled with cream.*

Marvellous Melon

Juicy, ripe and aromatic, melon is best eaten "raw" or as part of a fruit salad. Melon is one of the few fruits that appears to be universally popular. For a simple and pretty dessert, cut a round melon (charentais, galia or cantaloupe) in half horizontally and scoop out the seeds. The bowl-shaped shell makes a perfect container for fruit salad, ice cream or a fruit sauce. A sprinkling of ground ginger or chopped fresh mint also goes down well. The seeds can be dried and roasted in the oven to make a delicious snack.

Orange-fleshed cantaloupe or charentais melons are richer sources of vitamin C than the other varieties: a 100 g/3½ oz slice supplies more than half the RDA. These types also provide more beta-carotene, folate and vitamin B_{12}. All melons are low in calories due to their high water content.

ONE PORTION
A small slice

Maximize the nutrients

When buying a melon, look for one that feels heavy for its size and yields to gentle pressure at the stem end. It should also smell aromatic, but not too strong or musky as this is an indication of over-ripeness. Avoid melons with blemishes, soft patches, or an indented rind as this may be a sign

that the fruit has started to rot. To ripen a melon, keep it at room temperature until it begins to smell fragrant and feels slightly tender at the stem end. When cut, it is best stored in the fridge wrapped in cling film or in a polythene bag. Avoid buying ready-sliced fruit as the nutrient levels will have diminished. You can freeze melon, cut into cubes and placed in a freezer-proof bag, for up to three months.

HOW TO EAT MORE...

- *Thread cubes of feta or mozzarella cheese onto a skewer with a bite-sized piece of de-seeded watermelon.*
- *Blend honeydew or cantaloupe melon with honey, lime juice and mint or ground ginger to make a refreshing drink.*
- *Freeze slices of peeled melon, then purée in a food processor to make a delicious and refreshing granita.*
- *For a quick salad, arrange cubes of cooked chicken and melon in the centre of an iceberg lettuce leaf. Add a few halves of cherry tomato and a creamy mayonnaise dressing.*

FRUIT STICKS WITH CHOCOLATE DIP

This dessert is great fun to eat and you can adapt the recipe to include your child's favourite fruit. The wooden cocktail sticks can be removed if serving this to small children. Don't throw away the hollowed out half melon, you can make this dish more fun by sticking the fruit sticks into it until it's covered – like the prickles on a hedgehog.

3

SERVES 4

- ½ canteloupe melon, cut horizontally, seeds scooped out
- 1 mango, cut into bite-sized pieces
- 10 strawberries, sliced
- 1 tbsp lemon juice
- wooden cocktail sticks

For the chocolate sauce:

- 100 g/3½ oz good quality milk chocolate
- 150 ml/⅔ cup single cream
- 1–2 tbsp unrefined caster sugar, according to taste

1 Using a melon baller, scoop the flesh out of the melon and place it in a bowl. Put all the fruit into the bowl and toss in the lemon juice.

2 Thread the pieces of fruit onto the cocktail sticks.

4 To make the chocolate sauce, put the chocolate, cream and sugar in a heatproof bowl placed over a saucepan of gently simmering water. Gently heat

the chocolate, stirring occasionally, until melted. Leave to cool slightly, then pour into four individual dishes.

5 To serve, each person dips the fruit sticks into their own pot of chocolate sauce.

Plum Crazy

The perfect child-friendly fruit, plums nestle comfortably in a child's hand, making the fruit easy for kids to eat, and when at their peak, their juicy flesh needs no accompaniment. Plums are very versatile and can be transformed into delicious jams, mousses, fruit sauces and ice creams and added to crumbles, tarts, pies and cakes. They also fit neatly into a lunchbox.

Surprisingly, there are over 2000 varieties of plum, although we are only likely to see a handful of these in shops and markets. Some are best cooked, and others are delicious both cooked and as they come. Generally, dark-coloured plums have a slightly bitter skin and tart flavour, while the red and yellow varieties tend to be sweeter.

Plums are packed with immune-boosting anthocyanins, which are said to have wide-ranging disease-fighting capabilities and may protect the brain from the damaging effects of free radicals and toxins. They also contain quercetin, another potent free-radical fighter, along with potassium, essential for water balance and regulating normal blood pressure, and, surprisingly, vitamin E, which is great for healthy skin.

ONE PORTION
1–2 fresh plums

Maximize the nutrients

Plums are delicate and can easily become bruised, so look for unblemished fruit. Choose firm, plump plums that are very slightly under-ripe as they ripen fast and quickly pass their peak, which means that nutrients diminish. To preserve their nutrient levels store ripe plums in the fridge for one or two days at the most. When it comes to retaining their vitamin and mineral content it's best to serve plums uncooked. If stewing them, however, cook them briefly in a little water or natural fruit juice to retain as many of the nutrients as possible.

In their dried form plums become prunes (see pages 62–3), which are high in fibre and contain many minerals and are recognized for their ability to relieve constipation. The drying process concentrates the nutrients, particularly potassium and iron.

SWEET PLUM "PIZZA"

In this recipe I've used ready-made puff pastry. However, I've also made the base with pizza dough enriched with an egg yolk and sweetened with two tablespoons of caster sugar. It's delicious and makes a change from the usual cheese and tomato!

SERVES 4–6

- 40 g/1½ oz ground almonds
- 40 g/1½ oz caster sugar
- 1 free-range egg yolk
- 40 g/1½ oz unsalted butter
- 1 sheet puff pastry
- 1 free-range egg, beaten
- 6 red plums, pitted and sliced
- 2 tbsp plum or apricot jam
- milk for brushing

1 Preheat the oven to 200°C/ 400°F. In a mixing bowl, combine the ground almonds, caster sugar, egg yolk and butter until creamy. Chill.

2 Lay the pastry on a baking sheet and fold the edges over to make a 2 cm/¾ in lip. Brush the edges with milk.

3 Spread the almond cream over the pastry base, leaving a gap around the edge as it will ooze slightly during cooking, then arrange the plums on top.

4 Heat the jam with 1 tbsp water until it melts, then brush over the plums to give them a glossy shine. Bake the "pizza" for 20–25 minutes until the pastry is golden.

HOW TO EAT MORE...

- Plums and custard are a perfect match. Mix together 4 tbsp natural yogurt with the same amount of ready-made custard and serve with a sliced plum or two. To transform this into a breakfast dish, sprinkle with a spoonful of crunchy cereal and sunflower or pumpkin seeds. You could also leave out the custard and just use natural or flavoured yogurt.
- Pit and quarter plums and thread them onto skewers. Brush with honey and grill until tender.
- For a simple barbecue sauce, fry an onion and diced pitted plums in sunflower oil. Add brown sugar, a little white wine vinegar and water then cook until very tender. Purée or mash to a sauce consistency.
- Juice the plums and combine with peaches or nectarines to make a rich golden nectar.

Peaches & Nectarines

Often sweeter than peaches, nectarines are a richer source of vitamin C, which aids the absorption of iron, and is vital for healthy skin, bones and teeth. Lack of iron is associated with anaemia, mood swings, delays in development and poor concentration, and it is one nutrient many children lack, especially toddlers and teenage girls. Both fruits are good sources of beta-carotene.

Peaches and nectarines are very versatile, but you can't beat a juicy, ripe fruit served as it comes. They make deliciously creamy smoothies, luscious purées, ice creams and fools, simple pies and tarts, and can add a natural sweetness when stirred into curries, stews or pilaffs.

ONE PORTION
1 small to medium
peach or nectarine

Maximize the nutrients

Like peaches, nectarines do not continue to ripen after picking, so avoid rock-hard fruit. If the fruit is slightly firm, you can speed up the softening process by placing it in a paper bag with an already ripe fruit. Nectarines should be bright and smooth skinned, with no wrinkles or bruises. Peaches don't keep well, their delicate flesh soon deteriorates after ripening. Store them at room temperature for a few days, then keep them in the fridge. Nutritionally, peaches and nectarines are best left unpeeled, as much of their

vitamin C lies just under the skin.

Canned peaches in juice make a great standby, but lack the depth of flavour of the fresh fruit. The canning process also depletes around 80 percent of the vitamin C content.

KID PLEASING
If your child dislikes the fuzzy skin of the peach, they are easy to peel. Put the peach in a jug or bowl and pour over boiling water. Leave standing for about 30 seconds, then drain and refresh under cold running water. The skin will come off easily.

NECTARINE MELBA

The taste of this dessert depends on the use of perfectly ripe nectarines and raspberries, which also influence its vitamin content. Try to prepare as close to serving as possible, as vitamin levels will diminish after the fruit is cut or puréed.

2

SERVES 4

- 250 g/9 oz raspberries
- 1 tsp fresh lemon juice
- 2 tbsp icing sugar
- 4 ripe nectarines
- 8 scoops of good-quality vanilla ice cream, softened
- toasted flaked almonds, to decorate (optional)

1 To make the sauce, purée the raspberries in a blender and then press through a fine sieve to remove the seeds. Stir in the lemon juice and icing sugar.

Taste the sauce for sweetness – you may need to add a little more sugar.

2 Halve the nectarines along the natural groove and remove the stones. Put two nectarine halves on each serving plate. Place a scoop of ice cream in the hollow of each fruit.

3 Spoon over the raspberry sauce and sprinkle with almonds, if using.

HOW TO EAT MORE...

- *Stir small cubes of nectarine or peach into cooked couscous, bulghur wheat or brown rice, then sprinkle over toasted flaked almonds or pinenuts and drizzle with olive oil and lemon juice.*
- *To make individual portions of crumble, halve a peach or nectarine and remove the stone. Fill the cavity with a crumble mixture, then place the fruit in a buttered ovenproof dish. Bake in a 180°C/350°F oven for about 20 minutes until the crumble is golden.*
- *To make a tart, halve a peach or nectarine and remove the stone. Cut out 10 cm/4 in circles of puff pastry and place a nectarine or peach half cut-side-down in the centre of the pastry circle. Gently score the pastry around each fruit, without cutting right through. Melt some apricot jam or honey in a saucepan over a gentle heat, then brush a little jam over each piece of fruit. Place on a greased baking sheet and bake in a pre-heated 180°C/350°F oven for 20–25 minutes until the pastry is risen and golden.*

Mango & Papaya

These exotic fruits have an equally exotic flavour and appearance. The large, pear-shaped papaya, also known as paw paw, has a glorious orange-pink flesh and fragrant aroma, with small black seeds in the centre that have a peppery taste when dried, but are usually discarded.

The colour of mango skin ranges from green and yellow to orange and red, while the inside is a golden-orange colour. Fiddly to prepare because of its large, flat central stone and slippery flesh, the fruit can be peeled and the flesh sliced from around the stone or alternatively the skin can be scored and cubed using the method described in the "how to eat more" box on page 61. Don't waste the flesh left around the stone; for a real treat kids can suck any remaining fruit off the stone, but – be warned – the juice will run everywhere!

Ripe mangoes and papaya are best served very simply: sliced and sprinkled with a little lemon or lime juice; cubed in a fruit salad; or puréed to make a sauce for ice cream or a base for fools.

Slightly under-ripe fruit are commonly used in south-east Asian salads.

Papaya contains an enzyme called papain, which aids digestion and can be used to tenderize meat. However, don't use papaya in jelly as the papain will stop the jelly from setting. What both fruits have in common is a rich abundance of vitamin C and beta-carotene. Both nutrients are valuable antioxidants and will benefit hair, skin and nails.

ONE PORTION
A slice of mango
or papaya

Maximize the nutrients

A ripe papaya has a delicate scent and speckled yellow skin and gives slightly when pressed. It bruises easily, so should be handled with care to preserve the nutrient content.

Confusingly, the colour of a mango skin is not an indication of ripeness; some remain green when fully ripe. However, as with papaya, the skin of a ripe mango should yield slightly when pressed and is highly perfumed. Fruit that is not quite ripe should be left at room temperature until tender.

Both fruits are higher in vitamin C and beta-carotene when uncooked.

TRAFFIC LIGHT ICES

The red, orange and green of traffic lights are replicated here in frozen fruity stripes made up of puréed kiwi, mango and strawberries. The seeds in the kiwi fruit can be off-putting to some children, and they are not that easy to remove by sieving, so scoop out the central core first.

SERVES 4

- 250 g/9 oz strawberries, hulled
- icing sugar, to taste
- 1 mango
- 4 kiwi fruit, halved crossways

1 Purée the strawberries in a food processor or blender, then press through a sieve to remove any seeds. Taste and sweeten with icing sugar, as required. Spoon the purée into four ice-lolly moulds then freeze for about an hour until semi-solid.

2 Meanwhile, peel and slice the mango flesh and purée until smooth. Spoon the mango purée into the ice-lolly moulds on top of the semi-frozen strawberry purée. Return to the freezer for about 45 minutes until semi-solid.

3 Using a spoon, scoop out the kiwi seeds and discard, then scoop out the flesh. Blend to a purée, then press through a sieve to remove any stray seeds. Spoon the purée into the ice-lolly moulds and insert the lolly stick, depending on the type of mould you are using. Freeze the lollies until frozen.

HOW TO EAT MORE...

- *To peel a mango: hold the fruit with one hand and cut vertically down one side of the stone. Repeat on the opposite side. Taking the two large slices, cut the flesh into a criss-cross pattern down to the skin. Press each prepared mango half inside out and cut off the cubes of mango.*
- *Combine slices of mango or papaya with strips of cooked chicken or smoked ham and slices of cucumber. Dress with lemon juice and olive oil to make a refreshing salad.*
- *Simply purée mango or papaya and serve as a quick fruit sauce spooned over a fruit salad, meringue, ice cream or yogurt. These fruits also make an excellent base for smoothies or juices.*

Delicious Dried Fruits

The perfect high-energy, nutrient-dense snack; if your child balks at the sight of dried prunes and figs, he or she may find raisins, or dried apricots, mango, pineapple, peaches, bananas or apple rings more acceptable. The drying process concentrates the natural sugars found in the fruit as well as boosting the beta-carotene, soluble fibre, B vitamins, iron and potassium content. However, this is at the expense of vitamin C, which diminishes during the drying process. Bear in mind, though, that dried fruit is high in sugar and can contribute to tooth decay and gum disease.

Due to their high soluble fibre content, dried fruits – prunes and figs in particular – are a good natural choice for relieving constipation. Drinking a glass of prune juice, for example, at bedtime will encourage a bowel movement the next morning. Apart from being delicious, prunes are also very high in antioxidants, providing over twice as much as the antioxidant-rich fresh blueberry.

Avoid dried fruit that contains the preservative sulphur dioxide (E220), which has been found to trigger asthma attacks in some vulnerable people.

ONE PORTION
1 heaped
tablespoon

HOW TO EAT MORE...

- *Forget high-sugar, low-fruit jams, and make your own fruit spread. Place 200 g/7 oz dried chopped apricots, dates, mango, pineapple or peaches in a saucepan with 150 ml/5 fl oz fresh apple juice and 100 ml/3½ fl oz water. Bring to a boil and simmer for about 20 minutes until the fruit is very soft. Purée and set aside to cool.*
- *Stir chopped dried apricots, dates or apple into stuffing, nut roast or burger mixes. Or add to couscous, pilaffs, curries or stews.*
- *Make your own trail mix by combining chopped dried fruit with a selection of unsalted nuts and seeds.*

Maximize the nutrients

It is best to buy dried fruits in small quantities and store them in an airtight container. The beta-carotene, lycopene and soluble fibre content is made more available to the body when dried fruit is cooked.

STICKY DATE MUFFINS WITH TOFFEE SAUCE

These muffins are excellent served warm with the toffee sauce.

MAKES 10 MUFFINS

- 200 g/7 oz pitted dates, chopped
- 200 ml/7 fl oz water
- 1 tsp bicarbonate of soda
- 55 g/2 oz unsalted butter
- 175 g/6 oz self-raising flour
- 150 g/5½ oz caster sugar
- 1 tsp vanilla extract
- 2 free-range eggs, beaten
- 4 handfuls raspberries, to serve

For the toffee sauce:
- 142 ml/4½ fl oz double cream
- 1 tbsp golden syrup
- 70 g/2½ oz light brown sugar
- 55 g/2 oz unsalted butter

1 Preheat the oven to 180°C/ 350°F. Line a muffin tin with 10 large paper cases.

2 Put the dates in a pan with the water and bring to a boil. Cook for 10 minutes until softened. Stir in the bicarbonate of soda and butter. Stir until the butter has melted. Leave to cool then blend to make a rough purée.

3 Sift the flour into a mixing bowl. Using a wooden spoon, stir in the sugar, vanilla, eggs and date purée, until just combined. Divide the mixture between the muffin cases and bake for 20 minutes until risen and golden brown. Cool on a wire rack.

4 To make the toffee sauce, put the cream, syrup, sugar and butter in a small saucepan. Bring to the boil, stirring continuously, and simmer for about 10 minutes until thickened and glossy. Remove from the heat and leave to cool slightly.

5 Take the muffins from the paper cases and serve with the sauce and a handful of raspberries.

5

VEGETABLES

Colourful Carrots

Carrots really do have "superhero" qualities, as there's more than an element of truth in the old wive's tale that they help you see in the dark. This is thanks to the carrot's high levels of beta-carotene, which is converted into vitamin A in the body and is needed for good vision. Research has shown that just one carrot a day can help to improve night vision.

Carrots are one of several vegetables that kids seem to prefer raw – and they are certainly higher in vitamin C when uncooked. The crunchy texture and natural sweetness of uncooked carrots are infinitely preferable to even the lightly cooked or steamed alternative. If you're feeling creative, instead of sticks, try cutting carrots into different shapes.

Puréed carrots make perfect baby food, or can easily be sneaked into pasta sauces, soups and pie fillings for older children. Finely grated carrot almost disappears if incorporated into a home-made burger or a falafel mix and also makes a colourful addition to mixed salads and coleslaw (you could even add extra to shop-bought coleslaw). I also defy any child to identify carrot in a passion cake.

ONE PORTION
2–3 tablespoons

Maximize the nutrients

Look for firm, unwrinkled carrots – the smallest ones tend to be the sweetest. If you buy carrots with their feathery leaves on, it is best to remove them when you get home as they rob the root of nutrients. High pesticide residues have been found in carrots, so buy organic if you can. It's not essential to peel organic carrots, but if you buy non-organic, it's important to peel them and slice off the tops, which will remove most of the residues. Beta-carotene and fibre are more readily available when carrots are cooked, especially with a little fat.

HOME-MADE BURGERS

I've used minced organic beef to make these simple burgers, but you could use minced chicken, turkey, lamb or a vegetarian alternative.

MAKES 4

- 1 onion, grated
- 1 large carrot, finely grated
- 2 tbsp alfalfa sprouts
- 1 clove garlic, crushed
- 1 tsp dried oregano
- 30 g/1 oz fresh wholemeal breadcrumbs
- 375 g/13 oz lean minced organic beef
- 1 egg, beaten
- flour, for dusting
- salt and pepper
- olive oil, for frying

To serve:
- wholemeal burger buns, tomato, lettuce, chopped spring onions, humous, ketchup or mayonnaise

1 In a bowl, mix together the onion, carrot, alfalfa, garlic, oregano, breadcrumbs and mince. Season well, cover with cling film and chill for 30 minutes. Using floured hands, shape the mixture into 4 burgers.

2 Heat enough oil to lightly cover the base of a large frying pan.

Cook the burgers in two batches for about 4 minutes each side until golden.

3 To serve, split a burger bun in half then top with a burger, lettuce, tomato, onion and the condiment of your choice.

▼ HOW TO EAT MORE...

- *Make a nutritious breakfast drink by juicing carrots and apples.*
- *To make golden fairy cakes, line a muffin tin with 12 paper cases and preheat the oven to 180°C/350°F. Sift 225 g/8 oz self-raising flour with a pinch of salt and 2 tsp ground mixed spice. Stir in 225 g/8 oz soft light brown sugar and 225 g/8 oz grated carrots. Beat together 3 eggs and 175 ml/6 fl oz sunflower oil, then stir this into the flour mixture. Pour the mixture into the muffin cases and bake for about 25 minutes, until risen. For the icing, cream together 55 g/2 oz cream cheese and 30 g/1 oz butter until light and creamy. Beat in 40 g/1½ oz icing sugar and chill for 15 minutes. Using a small pointed knife and holding it at an angle, cut a cone of cake from the centre of each cooled muffin. Cut the cone in half to make two wings. Spoon the icing into the centre and perch the wings on top.*

Onions & Leeks

My daughter would happily polish off slices of raw onion as a toddler – and given the chance would still do so today. Unbeknown to her, she was doing herself a great deal of good. In natural medicine, onions are highly prized as one of the oldest remedies and a natural cure-all. In the past, an infusion of onions was often given to babies as a relief for colic.

ONE PORTION
2–3 tablespoons

Onions, leeks, spring onions, shallots and chives all have potent phytochemicals that may protect against cancer and heart disease. Raw or cooked, onions provide valuable amounts of fibre and have antiviral and antibacterial properties, helping to prevent colds, relieve bronchial congestion, asthma and hay fever. Onions may also protect against the effects of fatty foods on the blood. However, it is the presence of the antioxidant quercetin and its role in fighting cancer that is said to be most valuable, as it is more readily absorbed from onions than from other foods. Leeks have similar active constituents as onions, but also provide useful amounts of vitamin C and vitamin E.

Let's not forget the contribution that onions and leeks make to cooking. Both are indispensable, adding flavour and texture to a wide variety of savoury dishes and, if finely chopped, both are difficult to detect in many dishes. The milder flavour of leeks is excellent in soups, stews and pies, or steamed and served with a light creamy or cheesy sauce, or as part of a stir-fry.

Maximize the nutrients

Fresh, raw onions and leeks have the highest concentration of phytochemicals. Red onions have higher levels of quercetin than white.

When buying onions, choose ones that have a dry, papery skin and no sign of mould or softness. They will keep for a month in a cool, dark place. Try to buy leeks with their roots in tact, as they tend to deteriorate more quickly when the roots are removed. Ready-prepared or pre-washed leeks will also have lost some of their nutrients.

LEEK & POTATO SOUP

I make no apologies for including this all-time favourite. Here I've added crispy bacon bits, but this is optional. Croûtons, crispy fried onions or a sprinkling of grated Cheddar cheese are equally good.

SERVES 4

- 1 tbsp olive oil
- 4 leeks, sliced
- 1 stick celery, chopped
- 2 large carrots, chopped
- 3 medium potatoes, peeled and diced
- 1 bay leaf
- 1.2 litres/2 pints vegetable stock
- 3 tbsp crème fraîche or double cream
- 3 rashers bacon, grilled until crisp and chopped
- salt and pepper

1 Heat the olive oil in a large lidded saucepan and add the leeks. Fry over a medium heat for 5 minutes, until softened. Stir in the celery, carrots, potatoes and bay leaf and cook for another 5 minutes.

2 Add the stock and bring to the boil, then partially cover the pan and simmer for about 15–20 minutes. Transfer the vegetables to a blender and purée until smooth.

3 Return to the pan, season to taste and stir in the crème fraîche or cream. Heat through before serving topped with the bacon crisps.

▼

HOW TO EAT MORE...

- *When roasted, onions lose their pungency and develop a caramelized sweetness. Cut the onion – red onions are particularly good – into wedges and roast in a little olive oil for 30–35 minutes until tender and slightly blackened around the edges.*
- *To make cheesy stuffed baked potatoes, bake 4 potatoes for 1–1½ hours. Meanwhile, steam 2 chopped leeks. Cut each potato in half and scoop out the flesh. Mash with 40 g/1½ oz butter, 85 g/3 oz grated mature Cheddar cheese, 2 beaten eggs, the steamed leeks and seasoning. Spoon the mixture back into the potato skins and bake for 20 minutes.*
- *Add sautéed chopped spring onions to mashed potatoes, bread doughs, noodles and rice dishes.*

Rooting for Roots

Perfect comfort food, root vegetables are nourishing, filling and versatile. The sweet, dense flesh of turnips, parsnips, beetroot, swede and celeriac provides sustained energy, fibre and valuable amounts of vitamins and minerals.

For children, the sweet flavour of root vegetables is a significant attraction, and this sweetness is intensified when the vegetables are roasted. Beetroot develops a delicious caramelized stickiness when roasted – but boil it in its skin for around 20 minutes first to speed up the roasting.

The much-maligned turnip has a peppery flavour and is surprisingly rich in vitamin C and essential amino acids, such as lysine, which has been found to prevent cold sores. Baby turnips have a milder flavour and, again, are good roasted. Root vegetables are great mashed, and add substance to home-made or shop-bought soups. Casseroles and pies also benefit from the addition of root vegetables. However, they don't have to be restricted to hearty winter fare, as they are equally good grated raw into salads, instead of the usual coleslaw with cabbage and carrots.

ONE PORTION
2–3 tablespoons

Maximize the nutrients

Seek out firm, unwrinkled root vegetables with no soft patches, and store in a cool, dark place. Boiling affects the vitamin C and vitamin B levels, so steaming, microwaving and roasting are preferable. Cooking does increase the availability of beta-carotene and fibre. If you boil root vegetables, reserve the cooking water and use as the base for a stock.

HOW TO EAT MORE...

- Try combining different types of root vegetable with mashed potatoes. Swede, celeriac, parsnip, sweet potato and carrot are all suitable additions.
- Try making your own root vegetable crisps by thinly slicing beetroot, carrot, sweet potato, swede and parsnip. Deep-fry in sunflower oil until crisp, then drain on kitchen paper.
- Make root vegetable chips, slice into wedges, drizzle with olive oil and bake in a 200°C/400°F oven for about 30 minutes.
- Grate raw beetroot, celeriac or turnip and add to salads or coleslaw.

ROOT VEGETABLE NESTS

These rosti can be made the day before they are needed and stored in the fridge, layered between sheets of baking paper. They can also be shallow-fried rather than grilled.

MAKES 4 NESTS

- 550 g/1 lb 4 oz potatoes such as Maris Piper, unpeeled and halved
- 275 g/9½ oz turnip or celeriac, peeled and cut into large chunks
- 175 g/6 oz carrots, cut into large chunks
- 1 tbsp olive oil, plus more for brushing
- 1 large onion, thinly sliced
- salt and pepper
- 4 large free-range eggs
- rocket leaves, to serve

1 Boil the potatoes in a large saucepan of salted water for about 10 minutes until just tender. Drain, refresh in cold water, then leave to cool. Peel when cool.

2 Meanwhile, steam the turnip or celeriac and carrot chunks for about 4 minutes until just tender. Refresh in cold water, then leave to cool.

3 Heat the olive oil in a heavy-based saucepan and fry the onion for 10 minutes until softened, then set aside.

4 Preheat the grill to medium. When all the vegetables are cool, grate them into a bowl, stir in the onion and season.

5 Loosely form the mixture into 8 rosti, leaving the edges fairly ragged. Place the rosti on oiled baking sheets and brush the tops with more oil. Grill in two batches for about 15 minutes, turning once, until golden.

6 Meanwhile, boil the eggs for about 5 minutes, until the white is set but the yolk is runny.

7 Arrange the rosti on serving plates and scatter with a few rocket leaves. Shell the eggs, slice in half and place on top, then serve.

Super Squash!

The pumpkin is synonymous with Hallowe'en, when the centre is scooped out and the shell carved to make a jack-o'-lantern. Its decorative role is so prominent that we often forget that its sweet flesh can also be transformed into pie fillings and creamy soups, roasted or included in risottos and pasta dishes. All members of the pumpkin family are equally versatile – and nutritious.

Winter squashes come in all shapes, sizes and colours, and attractive single-portion squashes are now more readily available in supermarkets and greengrocers. They tend to have a sweeter flavour and make economic sense, for while pumpkins keep for months when whole, they need to eaten within a few days of being cut. Slice off the top, scoop out the seeds and fibres and roast them whole until meltingly tender. The smaller squashes also go well in dishes incorporating cream, cheese, tomatoes, nutmeg and bacon.

Boiling pumpkins, squashes and courgettes does little for their flavour. Already high in water, they simply absorb even more, ending up soggy and tasteless. Roasting, grilling and griddling are preferable, as these methods intensify the sweetness of the vegetables. Pumpkins and squashes rarely cause allergies and are easy to digest, making excellent weaning foods for babies.

The deep orange flesh provides plentiful amounts of beta-carotene, as well vitamins C and E, numerous B vitamins, magnesium, potassium and fibre. Butternut squash provides the highest amount of vitamin C out of all the winter squashes. Magnesium has been found to ease the symptoms of PMS and asthma, while B vitamins benefit the brain, mood and memory.

Don't forget to use pumpkin seeds too. Simply pick out the seeds, remove any stray fibres, and leave the seeds to dry, then roast them in a dry frying pan. Highly nutritious, pumpkin seeds are one of the few plant foods that provide both omega-3 and omega-6 essential fatty acids, along with iron, zinc, magnesium and vitamin E – all vital nutrients for the brain and concentration.

During the warmer months, summer squashes such as courgettes, marrow and cucumber come into their own. Small courgettes have the most

ONE PORTION
A handful or 2 tablespoons

flavour, although the refreshing juicy cucumber is probably the most popular with children out of the three. For packed lunches or snacks, slice the cucumber into 7 cm/2 in slices, scoop out the seeds and fill with cream cheese, humous or pâté.

Maximize the nutrients

Look for firm, bright, undamaged vegetables that are heavy for their size and have no soft patches. Winter squash can be kept for a few weeks if stored in a cool, dry place. Once cut, they can be kept in the fridge for a few days. Summer squash are more delicate and are best kept in the fridge for a few days only.

Cooking winter squash in a dish that contains a little oil will increase the availability of beta-carotene. Although B vitamins are lost if the squash are cooked in water.

▼

HOW TO EAT MORE...

- *Both finely chopped courgettes and bite-sized pieces of squash or pumpkin work well in risottos. Fry an onion until softened, add the vegetables and cook for another 3 minutes, then proceed according to the recipe. Finish off with plenty of freshly grated Parmesan cheese. You could also stir in a spoonful of basil pesto.*
- *Puréed or mashed butternut squash mixed with small pasta shapes, finely grated Parmesan and butter or olive oil is a popular weaning food in Italy.*
- *Steam finely grated courgettes for 1 minute then mix with finely chopped mint, a little olive oil and a squeeze of lemon juice.*
- *Cut pumpkin or squash into large bite-sized pieces and combine with wedges of onion and sausages on a lightly oiled roasting tray and cook in a 200°C/400°F oven for about 30 minutes, turning occasionally.*
- *Boil potatoes with butternut squash and a clove of garlic until tender. Drain and mash with milk and plenty of butter. Add seasoning to taste.*
- *Instead of boiling or steaming courgettes, slice them lengthways and griddle or grill them until tender and slightly blackened; this gives them a sweeter flavour.*
- *Grind up pumpkin seeds and add to smoothies, yogurts, breakfast cereals, flapjacks and breads. Toasted seeds make a convenient, healthy snack.*

Super Squash!

PUMPKIN FONDUE

A pumpkin shell makes a perfect container for a rich cheesy fondue. Use a selection of raw vegetables as tools to scoop out the fondue. This recipe will serve a family of four as a light lunch or starter with bread. Don't forget to eat the pumpkin!

2-3

SERVES 4

- 1 medium acorn squash or small pumpkin
- olive oil, for brushing
- 4 tbsp dry white wine
- 1½ tbsp cornflour
- 3 tbsp crème fraîche
- 175 g/6 oz Gruyère cheese, grated
- 1 clove garlic, crushed
- salt and pepper

To serve:
sticks of carrot, mange tout, baby corn, broccoli, cauliflower, celery, breadsticks, crisps, etc

1 Preheat the oven to 200°C/400°F. Slice off the top of the pumpkin and scoop out the seeds and any fibres. Brush the inside and top outer edge with oil and roast in the oven for 20 minutes until the flesh is almost tender.

2 Meanwhile, mix together the wine and cornflour, then add the crème fraîche, cheese and garlic. Season, then spoon the mixture into the hollowed-out pumpkin. Prop the pumpkin up using crumpled foil or baking paper and return it to the oven for 30 minutes until the fondue has risen and is golden on top.

3 Prepare the vegetables. Place the pumpkin in the centre of a serving plate and the crudités around the edge. When the fondue is finished eat the inside of the squash with a spoon.

MOROCCAN CHICKEN

It's good to encourage children to experience different flavours from an early age as they are less likely to be fussy eaters later in life. This couscous dish is lightly flavoured with cumin and coriander and is a perfect introduction to spicy foods. Adults may like to spice it up by adding some chopped fresh chilli.

2-3

SERVES 4

- 225 g/8 oz couscous
- hot chicken or vegetable stock, to cover
- 25 g/1 oz unsalted butter
- 1½ tbsp olive oil
- 1 large onion, finely chopped
- 3 skinless chicken breasts, cut into bite-sized pieces
- ½ orange pepper, seeded and finely chopped
- 2 courgettes, diced
- 2 cloves garlic, crushed

- 2 tsp ground cumin
- 2 tsp ground coriander
- 1 tsp paprika
- 100 g/3½ oz dried apricots or dates, finely chopped
- 55 g/2 oz pine nuts, toasted
- salt and pepper
- fresh coriander, chopped, to garnish (optional)

1 Place the couscous in a bowl and cover with 1 cm/½ in hot stock. Stir the couscous and leave to stand for about 10 minutes until the stock has been absorbed. Fluff up the couscous with a fork.

2 Heat the butter and oil in a heavy-based saucepan and fry the onion for about 8 minutes, stirring frequently, until softened and light brown.

3 Add the chicken and cook for 4 minutes, stirring occasionally, until golden. Add the pepper, courgettes, garlic, cumin, coriander and apricots and cook for a further 5 minutes, stirring, until the chicken is cooked through and the vegetables are tender.

4 Gently stir in the couscous and warm through over a low heat. Season to taste and serve sprinkled with pine nuts and coriander, if using.

Amazing Avocado

My children were weaned on avocado and this highly nutritious "fruit" makes a perfect first food: it doesn't require cooking, comes in its own natural packaging and is quick and simple to prepare. It wasn't that long ago that avocados were scorned for their high fat content. Today, health guidelines encourage us to eat more of them.

Nutritionally, avocados are almost a complete food, supplying small amounts of protein and carbohydrate as well as beneficial monounsaturated oil. They also contain the highest concentration of the antioxidant vitamin E of any fruit, as well as eye-protecting lutein, some B vitamins, vitamin C, folic acid, potassium and iron – a deficiency of which has been linked to fatigue, depression and poor digestion. This nutritious combination is also known to help improve the condition of skin and hair.

For children, serving an avocado halved with the stone removed and the cavity filled with a simple vinaigrette dressing made with either lemon juice or balsamic vinegar and extra-virgin olive oil is more fun than when it's sliced – all that's needed is a spoon to scoop out the flesh. But you can't beat a creamy, garlicky guacamole filling: add some finely chopped red pepper or tomato to increase the vegetable count (and a spoonful of mayonnaise, while not entirely authentic, gives a creamier result).

Prawns go very well with avocado, and a favourite in my house is the good old prawn cocktail, made with prawns, mayonnaise, a little ketchup, lemon juice and a dash of paprika, piled on top of an avocado half.

ONE PORTION
½ medium avocado

Maximize the nutrients

Try to serve avocado as soon as possible after preparing it as avocado flesh turns brown when it comes into contact with air. To prevent this, brush the cut surface with lemon juice, which will also help to preserve the nutrients. To keep the colour of an avocado dip, bury the stone from the centre of the fruit in the middle of the dip and cover the bowl with clingfilm. Don't forget to remove the stone before serving.

CHICKEN FAJITAS WITH GUACAMOLE

This makes a quick and satisfying after-school meal.

SERVES 4

- 1 tbsp olive oil, plus extra for brushing
- 4 chicken breasts, about 115 g/4 oz each, cut into strips
- 1 red onion, sliced
- 1 red pepper, seeded and sliced
- 1 clove garlic, crushed
- 1 tsp ground cumin
- juice of 1 lime
- 4 soft tortillas, to serve

For the guacamole:
- 1 large avocado, stone removed and flesh scooped out
- 1 clove garlic, crushed
- juice of ½ lemon
- 1 tomato, seeded and finely chopped (optional)
- 1 tbsp mayonnaise
- salt and pepper

1 To make the guacamole, put all the ingredients into a bowl and mash with a fork until creamy. Set aside.

2 Heat a griddle pan, brush with oil and add the chicken. Cook for 6–8 minutes, turning once, until cooked through. Add the onion and pepper and griddle until softened.

3 Heat the oil in a small saucepan and cook the garlic and cumin for 1 minute. Add the lime juice and heat through.

4 Warm the tortillas, and add a spoonful of the chicken mixture to each. Spoon the spiced oil over and add a spoonful of guacamole before serving.

2-3

HOW TO EAT MORE...

- *To make a creamy salad dressing, blend an avocado with the juice of a lime or ½ lemon, 3 tbsp of fromage frais and one tbsp of chopped fresh coriander, mint or basil.*
- *Use in place of butter in sandwiches, blend ½ avocado with a little mayonnaise until creamy, and spread.*
- *Halve an avocado and remove the stone. Brush with lemon juice and fill the cavity with crème fraîche mixed with grated mature Cheddar and grilled bacon bits. Sprinkle with breadcrumbs and bake in a 200°C/400°F oven for 12–14 minutes until golden on top.*

Brilliant Broccoli

A powerhouse of nutrients and goodness, the health benefits of broccoli mean little to most children, as it's the taste that is usually the first hurdle parents have to overcome. However, once overcome, you'll have a broccoli lover for life!

Interestingly, young children have more tastebuds than adults and consequently their palates are heightened, so broccoli can taste quite bitter to them. This bitterness is also influenced by temperature. Even to broccoli lovers, cold broccoli tastes pretty offensive. Since children tend to leave their least favourite part of a meal to last, chances are it's going to be cold. I sometimes serve up broccoli slightly after the other components of the meal, so even if it is left to last it still retains some warmth. Alternatively, combining a bitter food with dairy produce can help to tame any bitterness.

One thing in broccoli's favour in terms of kiddie appeal is its shape. I'm sure many of us have used the "try some of the little tree" technique, but it does seem to work,

especially if the meal as a whole has a "garden" theme. Don't forget the stalks too, since these are also nutritious. Strangely enough, my daughter is more than happy to eat the stalks but fights shy of the floret, while my son likes the floret and avoids the stalk! I've also found that organic broccoli tastes much better than non-organic.

ONE PORTION
A handful or 1 medium-sized floret

Maximize the nutrients

Steaming and stir-frying are preferable cooking methods to boiling, which depletes water-soluble nutrients such as folate and vitamin C. Over-cooked broccoli has little going for it in terms of taste or nutrients, so it's pretty much a no-no. Boiling broccoli tends to turn the florets into mush, but steaming, stir-frying or microwaving helps to retain both the flavour and the precious health benefits. Serve broccoli when the stalks are just tender but not soft.

Raw broccoli contains almost as much calcium as milk, and the mineral is not totally diminished through cooking. Kids often prefer raw vegetables to cooked and as long as the broccoli is young and fresh, the stalks and florets are perfect for dipping into humous, mayonnaise, creamy cheese dip or guacamole.

Researchers have found that the phytochemicals in broccoli are especially valuable in stimulating the body's natural disease-fighting abilities, particularly against cancer of the lung, colon, breast and prostate. Latest studies show that by serving broccoli and tomatoes together you increase the cancer-fighting qualities. Other impressive attributes include numerous B vitamins, iron, zinc, potassium, and fibre. Ideally, broccoli should be part of your child's regular weekly diet.

HOW TO EAT MORE...

- *A smooth, rich cheese sauce will help to disguise any traces of bitterness in the broccoli. Try combining broccoli with leeks, cauliflower and pasta. Pour the cheese sauce over, then sprinkle over whole wheat breadcrumbs combined with finely chopped nuts and seeds. Grill until the top is crisp and golden.*

- *Purée steamed broccoli and stir into mashed potatoes with garlic, cheese and olive oil for an alternative to ordinary mashed potatoes or as a dip, or spread over flour tortillas or pitta bread. Top with slices of cooked chicken, or tuna or prawns.*

- *Broccoli stalks (as long as they are quite young and fresh) taste just as good as the florets and are often easier to incorporate into dishes such as coleslaw. Grate the broccoli stalks and combine with grated carrot and white cabbage, then stir in sliced spring onions, mayonnaise and lemon juice.*

- *Stir-fried broccoli retains a delicious crunch and goes well with black bean sauce or a splash of soy sauce.*

BROCCOLI & PARMESAN FRITTERS

These light, cheesy fritters incorporate finely chopped pieces of broccoli and sweet kernels of corn. They don't take long to prepare and make use of canned corn, but if in season fresh corn-on-the-cob is perfect. Just slice the kernels off the hard cob with a sharp knife. Serve with carrot and red pepper sticks to boost the vegetable count.

MAKES 12 FRITTERS

- 250 g/9 oz broccoli florets with stalks
- 200 g/7 oz canned no-sugar or salt sweetcorn, drained well
- 55 g/2 oz freshly grated Parmesan cheese
- 2 eggs, beaten
- 4 tbsp unbleached flour
- sunflower oil, for frying
- salt and pepper

1 Steam the broccoli for 3 minutes, until just tender, drain well, then finely chop the florets and stalks. Leave to cool.

2 Mix the broccoli with the sweetcorn, Parmesan, eggs and flour in a bowl and lightly season to taste.

3 Heat enough oil to cover the bottom of a heavy-based frying pan. Add 2 heaped tbsp of the mixture for each fritter and cook three fritters at a time. Cook for 2–3 minutes each side, until set and golden. Drain on paper towels and keep warm while you cook the remaining fritters.

"HULK" PASTA

The suggestion that food makes you big and strong goes down well with children, particularly boys! Much as I dislike the use of cartoon characters to sell sugary and fatty foods, it can be a useful technique to use at times.

This pasta dish comes with a fresh pesto sauce but you could use ready-made. The small florets of broccoli nestle hidden in the pasta!

2

SERVES 4

For the pesto:
- 55 g/2 oz fresh basil
- 2 cloves garlic, chopped
- 40 g/1½ oz pinenuts
- 125 ml/4 fl oz olive oil
- 4 tbsp freshly grated Parmesan cheese
- salt and pepper

For the pasta:
- 300 g/10½ oz tagliatelle
- 175 g/6 oz no-sugar or salt canned cannellini beans, drained
- 225 g/8 oz broccoli, cut into small florets
- 2 tbsp pinenuts, lightly toasted
- 2 tbsp freshly grated Parmesan cheese

1 To make the pesto, put the basil, garlic and pinenuts in a blender or food processor and process until finely chopped. Gradually add the oil, followed by the Parmesan to make a coarse purée. Season to taste.

2 Cook the pasta following the package instructions. Add the beans 1 minute before the end of the cooking time and heat through. Drain, reserving 3 tbsp of the cooking water. Return the pasta and beans to the pan.

3 Meanwhile, steam the broccoli for about 4–5 minutes or until just tender.

4 Add the broccoli to the pasta. Stir in the pesto and reserved cooking water, then season. Serve sprinkled with pinenuts and Parmesan.

Splendid Spinach

Popeye, who gulped down cans of spinach to gain super strength, was a big influence on the healthy image of this vegetable. Unfortunately, spinach doesn't actually contain a huge amount of iron in a usable form, but it is a rich source of natural plant compounds, phytochemicals, carotenoids, folic acid and vitamin C – it contains about four times more beta-carotene than broccoli.

Many children dislike the soggy texture and bitterness of cooked spinach. Raw baby spinach leaves are one of the most nutritious salad leaves and have a milder flavour than when cooked. I've recently discovered the wonders of frozen chopped spinach, which comes in handy little blocks. During the freezing process, spinach seems to lose any trace of bitterness and no preparation is needed. I've managed to add a block or two to pasta sauces, rice dishes, stir-fried noodles and curry without any sign of dissent or disapproval – but you'll have to gauge how much you can get away with.

ONE PORTION
A handful of leaves or 2 tablespoons

Maximize the nutrients

Raw is best when it comes to retaining levels of vitamins C and B. However when lightly cooked, stir-fried or steamed, the eye-protecting anti-oxidant lutein, beta-carotene and protein can be converted into a more usable form. The body will absorb more of the iron found in spinach if it is served with a vitamin C-rich food such as tomatoes or a glass of orange juice. Store for up to 3 days in the fridge.

HOW TO EAT MORE...

- *For mini eggs Florentine, steam 250 g/9 oz young leaf spinach until wilted. Squeeze out any excess water. Finely chop the spinach and mix with 4 tbsp crème fraîche and a little grated nutmeg. Season and spoon the mixture into 4 ramekins. Break an egg into each ramekin and sprinkle with grated Cheddar cheese. Bake for 10 minutes in a 180°C/350°F oven.*
- *Add finely chopped steamed spinach to pesto sauce.*
- *Mix a spinach purée into bread dough.*
- *Combine baby spinach leaves with other salad leaves, such as watercress or Cos as well as slices of avocado, grilled bacon and pear to create an invigorating, healthy salad.*

FLORENTINE BAKED GNOCCHI

I've used frozen chopped spinach to make this comforting, warming dish, although you can use shredded raw leaves. The tomato and cheese sauce will tame any hint of bitterness in the vegetable.

SERVES 4

- 650 g/1 lb 7 oz potato gnocchi
- 100 g/3½ oz frozen chopped spinach, defrosted
- 150 g/5½ oz mozzarella cheese, drained and cubed
- 55 g/2 oz Parmesan cheese, grated
- salt and pepper

For the tomato sauce:
- 1 tbsp olive oil
- 1 large onion, chopped
- 1 large clove garlic, chopped
- 1 tsp dried oregano
- 1 glass dry white wine (optional)
- 700 g/1 lb 9 oz jar of passata
- 1 tbsp tomato purée
- pinch of sugar

1 Preheat the oven to 180°C/ 350°F.

2 To make the tomato sauce, heat the oil in a large heavy-based saucepan and fry the onion over a medium-low heat for 10 minutes until softened. Add the garlic and oregano and cook for another minute, then pour in the wine, if using. Increase the heat and cook until the wine has almost evaporated.

3 Add the passata, tomato purée and sugar and cook over a medium-low heat for about 10 minutes, until reduced and thickened. Season to taste.

4 Cook the gnocchi in boiling salted water for 1½ minutes.

5 Drain the gnocchi well and add it with the spinach to the tomato sauce. Stir gently until well combined then transfer to a large, ovenproof dish. Scatter over the mozzarella cheese and top with Parmesan cheese, then bake for 20–25 minutes, until golden on top.

Powerful Peas

Peas are one of the few vegetables that taste just as good frozen as fresh – and nutritionally frozen peas are often richer in nutrients. This is because freezing takes place soon after picking, ensuring optimum freshness and nutrient levels, which readily diminish if fresh peas are stored for too long. However, peas are blanched before they are frozen and this process reduces the vitamin C and thiamine content. Opt for petit pois, which have a delicate sweet flavour and tender outer skin.

If you can find *really* fresh fresh peas, get the children involved in popping them out of their pods. This is a great way of involving kids in cooking – and raw fresh peas taste pretty good too!

Peas provide a good source of protein and iron – making them a good choice for vegetarians and vegans – as well as thiamine (vitamin B$_1$), folate, vitamin C, phosphorus and potassium.

ONE PORTION
2–3 tablespoons

HOW TO EAT MORE...

- *Pea purée makes a nutritious accompaniment to sausages, fish and burgers. Flavour the peas with some fried onion and mint and purée in a blender with a spoonful of cream or crème fraîche.*
- *For a great pea soup all you need is a bag of frozen peas, chopped onion, celery and carrot, a bay leaf and vegetable stock. When the vegetables are cooked, whizz the mixture in a blender. Add milk, cream or crème fraîche if you want a creamier soup.*
- *Stir cooked peas into risotto or pasta sauce made with garlic and herb cream cheese and grilled bacon.*
- *Mash cooked peas into home-made or shop-bought guacamole.*

Maximize the nutrients

Lightly steamed or microwaved peas contain a higher concentration of nutrients than boiled peas, as these cooking methods help to preserve water-soluble B vitamins and heat-sensitive vitamin C. When buying frozen peas, check the "use-by" date on the packet and feel the packet to ensure that the peas are not stuck together in clumps as this is a sign that they may have defrosted at some stage then refrozen, resulting in a loss of vitamin C as well as being a danger to health.

EASY-PEASY STARFISH PIE

The puff pastry fish and starfish add fun to this classic fish pie, although you could top the pie with mashed potato instead. Hard-boiled egg and prawns can be added to the sauce.

SERVES 4–6

- 1 tbsp olive oil
- 2 leeks, finely sliced
- 1 large carrot, finely chopped
- 150 g/5½ oz frozen petit pois
- 2 tbsp plain flour, plus extra for dusting
- 568 ml/1 pint warm milk
- 2 tsp Dijon mustard
- 2 tbsp finely chopped fresh parsley (optional)
- squeeze of fresh lemon juice
- 85 g/3 oz mature Cheddar cheese, grated
- 450 g/1 lb undyed smoked haddock, skinned and boned, cut into pieces
- 300 g/10½ oz cod fillet, skinned and boned, cut into pieces
- 1 sheet ready-rolled puff pastry, defrosted if frozen
- 1 egg, beaten
- salt and pepper

1 Preheat the oven to 200°C/ 400°F. Heat the oil in a large, heavy-based saucepan and fry the leeks for 5 minutes, until softened. Add the carrot and cook for a further 3 minutes, then stir in the peas.

2 Add the flour and stir continuously for about 2 minutes until the vegetables are coated, then gradually add the milk, stirring well between each addition until you have a smooth, thick white sauce. Mix in the mustard, parsley (if using) and lemon juice, then add the cheese and stir well until it has melted. Season to taste, making sure you don't add too much salt as the haddock is already quite salty.

3 Place the haddock and cod in a large ovenproof dish. Pour over the vegetable sauce until the fish is evenly covered and mix gently.

4 Place the pastry on a lightly floured work surface. Using pastry cutters, make fish and starfish shapes, then arrange them on top of the fish pie. Brush the pastry shapes with the beaten egg and bake for about 25 minutes, until the fish is cooked through and the pastry shapes have risen and are golden brown.

Crunchy Cauliflower

I must admit cauliflower is not a vegetable I buy on a regular basis but since experimenting with new ideas I am pleasantly surprised by its versatility and ability to merge with other flavours – and it's super-nutritious too. Immersing the creamy white florets in a cheese sauce is a popular option, but cauliflower is also good when flavoured with spices in a curry, combined with other vegetables in a stew, puréed as a side vegetable or in a soup, in salads with a light vinaigrette dressing and raw as a scoop for dips. Like other cruciferous vegetables, cauliflower has a slightly bitter flavour, a taste that is heightened in children with their more sensitive palates. Dairy foods such as cheese and milk will soften any bitterness, hence the popularity of cauliflower cheese. Cauliflower also contains sulphurous

ONE PORTION
A handful or a
medium-sized floret

compounds, which are the reason for the unpleasant smell it releases during cooking. Steaming in a covered pan creates a build-up of sulphur, which can taint the taste, but fast boiling in a minimal amount of water until the florets are just tender will reduce this build-up without losing too many valuable nutrients.

One thing in cauliflower's favour is its shape – and the fact that it's not green. We've all used the "little tree" technique when it comes to serving broccoli, but it works equally well with cauliflower florets – just think snow-covered trees!

Maximize the nutrients

Cauliflower is a rich source of nutrients and, like the other cruciferous vegetables, contains a cocktail of anti-carcinogenic properties. These are maximized when the vegetable is served raw, microwaved, stir-fried or lightly cooked. Don't forget the stalks, too, which also contain valuable nutrients. Avoid cauliflower with black spots or yellowing leaves and store in the refrigerator for up to 3 days.

CHEESY VEGETABLE BITES

Florets of cauliflower and broccoli as well as carrot batons are dipped in a light cheesy batter and deep-fried to make crisp vegetable bites – perfect as a vegetable accompaniment or main dish if served with a tomato salsa and salad. Mushrooms, aubergine, courgette and onion can also be used here.

SERVES 4

- 325 g/11½ oz cauliflower and broccoli florets
- 2 large carrots, cut into thick sticks or batons
- sunflower oil, for frying

For the cheese batter:
- 50 g/1¾ oz plain flour, sifted
- 50 g/1¾ oz Parmesan cheese, finely grated
- 150 ml/5 fl oz milk
- 1 egg, beaten
- salt

1 In a bowl, beat together the ingredients for the cheese batter. Season with salt and set aside.

2 Steam the cauliflower, broccoli and carrots for about 3 minutes until tender. Refresh under cold running water, drain well, and leave to cool slightly.

3 Heat plenty of oil in a deep saucepan. Dip the vegetables in the batter and deep-fry in batches for about 2–3 minutes, until golden. Drain on kitchen paper before serving.

HOW TO EAT MORE...
- *Steam 225 g/8 oz cauliflower until just tender. Fry a small onion and a clove of chopped garlic until softened. Purée the cauliflower, onion and garlic with 175 ml/6 fl oz vegetable stock and 2 tbsp crème fraîche, then season. Combine this purée with regular mashed potatoes or serve on its own as an accompaniment to meat or fish.*
- *Follow the recipe for Broccoli fritters (see page 80) but use cauliflower instead. You could also add a handful of cold cooked rice to bulk out the mixture.*
- *To boost the vegetable content of cauliflower cheese, add lightly steamed leeks, broccoli and carrots to the sauce and top with sliced tomato and breadcrumbs before baking.*

Bold Brassicas

As members of the brassica family, cabbage and Brussels sprouts undoubtedly win the title of "most disliked vegetables". This is unjust, since prepared in the right way they can actually taste pretty good – honestly! I'm convinced that much of the dislike stems from ingrained prejudice or the barriers put up by parents who remember being served overcooked, sloppy cabbage and sprouts as children. It's all too easy to avoid giving kids cabbage and sprouts believing they're not going to like them ... so why bother?

However, there is a good scientific reason why young children turn their noses up at these vegetables. Like broccoli, cabbage and sprouts have bitter undertones that are heightened when eaten by small children as their tastebuds are particularly sensitive to such flavours. I've found white or red cabbage is most acceptable, especially when served raw shredded into coleslaw, or finely shredded and lightly cooked in a stir-fry. A little soy sauce or black bean sauce is a useful cover up. Alternatively, try stirring finely chopped steamed cabbage into mashed potatoes or adding it to pie fillings, bakes or stews.

Kids seem to either love or loathe Brussels sprouts. They resemble baby cabbages and, like their big brothers, they are best when lightly cooked, shredded into stir-fries or, as some parents I've talked to suggest, obliterated by gravy. Combining sprouts or cabbage with sweeter vegetables such as carrot, sweet potato, sweetcorn and red pepper helps to counter any bitterness, as does cooking them with dairy products – such as baking them in a cheese sauce with macaroni and other vegetables, for example.

Reassuringly, a portion is really quite small at just two tablespoons, so piling cabbage onto a child's plate is not only off-putting but also unnecessary.

In their favour, cabbage and sprouts contain a wealth of vitamins and minerals along with cancer-fighting properties and antioxidant capabilities. Perhaps surprisingly, Brussels sprouts contain four times the amount of vitamin C found in cabbage.

ONE PORTION
2 tablespoons

Maximize the nutrients

Cabbage and sprouts need to be handled with care if the nutrients are to be preserved. Over half of their vitamin C content is lost when these vegetables are boiled, with slightly higher amounts retained when they are steamed or microwaved. The dark green outer leaves of Savoy cabbage are more nutritious than the paler leaves found towards the centre. Raw is best, however, and numerous studies have highlighted cabbage's potent antiviral and antibacterial properties. If you do boil your vegetables, a drop of olive oil in the cooking water is said to increase the bioavailability of the beta-carotene. Also, don't throw away the cooking water, it will make a nutritious base for a vegetable stock.

HOW TO EAT MORE...

- *Sauté halved sprouts in olive oil then sprinkle with crisp breadcrumbs mixed with finely grated Parmesan cheese.*
- *Finely shredded Savoy cabbage can be baked in a foil parcel with a little butter and caraway seeds.*
- *Garlic butter goes well with both sprouts and cabbage.*
- *Chop and steam finely chopped cabbage or sprouts and add to mashed potatoes with sautéed spring onions.*
- *Stir-fry finely shredded cabbage or sprouts with garlic, ginger, red pepper, spring onions and carrot. Add fresh apple juice and a splash of soy sauce.*
- *Add shredded cabbage or sprouts to potato rosti or potato cakes.*
- *Cabbage leaves make the perfect wrap for rice, fish or other vegetables.*
- *Add finely chopped white or red cabbage to a meatball, burger or nut roast mix.*

SUNFLOWER POWER

The crunchy home-made coleslaw forms the centre of these pretty sunflowers. These make a perfect light lunch or tea.

SERVES 4

- 1 tbsp sunflower seeds
- 1 red-skinned apple, grated
- ½ tbsp lemon juice
- 55 g/2 oz white cabbage, grated
- 1 large carrot, grated
- 1 spring onion, finely chopped
- 55 g/2 oz Cheddar cheese, diced

For the dressing:
- 1 tbsp extra-virgin olive oil
- ½ tbsp lemon juice
- 2 tbsp mayonnaise

To serve:
lightly salted tortilla chips, long cucumber sticks and sugar snap peas

1 Toast the sunflower seeds in a dry frying pan until lightly golden. Leave to cool.

2 Toss the apple in the lemon juice to prevent it from browning. In a bowl, mix the apple together with the cabbage, carrot, spring onion and cheese.

3 To make the dressing, mix together the oil and the lemon juice, then add the mayonnaise and stir well until combined. Spoon over the coleslaw.

4 Arrange a heaped round of coleslaw in the centre of four plates, then sprinkle over the sunflower seeds. Place the tortilla chips around the coleslaw for flower petals, add sticks of cucumber for the stalk and sugar snap peas for the leaves.

CRUNCHY VEGETABLE CRUMBLE

The cheesy, crisp crumble topping hides a multitude of finely chopped vegetables. I like to serve this in individual dishes but you can cook it in a large ovenproof dish instead. The filling when blended makes an excellent baby purée. Serve with steamed sugar snap peas.

SERVES 4–6

- 1 tbsp olive oil
- 450 g/1 lb potatoes, quartered if large
- 1 large onion, finely chopped
- 1 red pepper, seeded and finely chopped
- 1 clove garlic, chopped
- 1 tsp dried mixed herbs
- 200 g/7 oz Savoy cabbage or Brussels sprouts, finely chopped
- 1 large parsnip, peeled and grated
- 1 large carrot, peeled and grated
- 400 ml/14 fl oz vegetable stock
- 200 ml/7 fl oz milk
- salt and pepper

For the crumble:
- 100 g/3½ oz plain flour
- 2 tsp mustard powder
- 85 g/3 oz cold unsalted butter, diced
- 85 g/3 oz Brazil nuts, finely chopped
- 100 g/3½ oz Cheddar cheese, grated

1 Preheat the oven to 180°C/375°F. Boil the potatoes in plenty of boiling salted water until just tender. Drain and peel, then set aside.

2 Heat the oil in a large, heavy-based saucepan and fry the onion over a medium heat for 8 minutes. Add the pepper, garlic and mixed herbs and cook for another 2 minutes.

3 Add the cabbage or Brussels sprouts, parsnip, carrot and cooked potatoes and cook, stirring frequently, for 5 minutes. Pour in the stock and milk, season and heat through. You can half-blend the mixture at this stage if a smoother filling is preferred. Divide the mixture between 6 large ramekins or moulds.

4 To make the crumble, mix together the flour and mustard powder, then rub in the butter using your fingertips until the mixture forms coarse crumbs with some larger chunks. Stir in the nuts and cheese.

5 Sprinkle the crumble over the filling then bake for 20 minutes until the top is slightly golden and crisp.

Beans & Pods

Pods such as mange tout and sugar snap peas are at their best when lightly cooked or, even better, raw, when they can be eaten pod and all.

French, runner and dwarf beans need to be cooked (unless you find very young beans in season) until just tender. A squeeze of lemon juice, drizzle of olive oil or dollop of butter – better still, garlic butter – add extra interest.

When young and fresh, broad beans taste sweet and delicate. Steam or boil them in a little water until tender. Older beans have a tough outer skin that is best removed to reveal a vibrantly coloured green bean with a soft texture.

Beans and pods provide a range of nutrients, including vitamins C and E, beta-carotene, iron, thiamine, folate, phosphorus and potassium.

ONE PORTION
2–3 tablespoons

Maximize the nutrients

Look for fresh, bright green, plump young beans and pods for the highest concentration of nutrients. Lightly steaming, microwaving or stir-frying are the best cooking methods, as boiling reduces the vitamin C content. Raw beans contain the most nutrients, although cooking will increase the availability of protein and fibre found in the beans. Broad beans retain most of their nutrients when frozen, but canning reduces the vitamin C count. Fresh beans and pods will keep in the fridge for two days.

HOW TO EAT MORE...

- *Transform cooked broad beans into a delicious dip. Combine the beans with crushed garlic, olive oil, finely chopped mint and lemon juice and blend until smooth and creamy. Alternatively purée and add to guacamole.*
- *Stir-fry mange tout, yellow pepper, carrot sticks and slices of chicken in hoisin sauce. Serve in an omelette wrap.*
- *Instead of salmon kebabs (see right), pile the rice in the centre of a plate and arrange strips of omelette around the edge in a circle to make a shining sun.*

CHINESE RICE WITH SALMON KEBABS

The honey-glaze gives these salmon kebabs a delicious glossy coating, but do take care when giving them to young children. Soak the wooden skewers in water for 30 minutes to prevent them from burning.

SERVES 4

4 x salmon fillets, about 500 g/ 1 lb 2 oz total weight, skinned and cut into 2 cm/¾ in cubes
- 250 g/9 oz brown rice
- 600 ml/20 fl oz water
- 1 tbsp sunflower oil
- 1 tsp toasted sesame oil
- 2 cloves garlic, finely chopped
- 2.5 cm/1 in piece fresh root ginger, peeled and grated
- 1 large red pepper, seeded and thinly sliced
- 8 baby corn, sliced into rounds
- 200 g/7 oz sugar snap peas
- 2 tbsp soy sauce
- 3 tbsp fresh apple juice

For the marinade:
- 2 tbsp runny honey
- 2 tbsp soy sauce
- 2 tbsp sunflower oil
- 1 tsp toasted sesame oil

1 In a shallow dish, mix together the ingredients for the marinade. Add the salmon and stir until the fish is fully coated. Leave to marinate for at least an hour, turning occasionally. Divide the salmon between 8 wooden skewers.

2 Put the rice in a saucepan and cover with water until it is covered by about 2 cm/¾ in. Bring to the boil, reduce the heat, cover, and simmer for about 30 minutes until the water has been absorbed and the rice is tender. Remove from the heat and leave to stand, covered, for 5 minutes.

3 Preheat the grill to high. Meanwhile, heat the oils in a large heavy-based frying pan. Add the garlic, ginger, red pepper, corn and sugar snap peas and stir-fry for about 8 minutes, stirring and tossing frequently.

4 Line the grill rack with foil and place the skewers on top. Brush the salmon with the marinade and grill for 3–5 minutes, turning occasionally.

5 Add the soy sauce, apple juice and rice to the frying pan – you may need to add a little extra liquid if it looks too dry. Stir until the rice has warmed through.

6 Divide the rice between 4 shallow bowls and top with the salmon kebabs.

Aubergine Appeal

Roasted, grilled, baked, puréed, there really isn't much you can't do with aubergines – except eat them raw. They get a mixed reaction from children, but I've found peeling them to remove the slightly tough purple skin makes them more acceptable. Their mild flavour makes them perfect when cooked with stronger-flavoured ingredients such as onions, garlic and tomatoes as in the classic ratatouille, moussaka and aubergine parmigiana. Finely chopped and cooked in a pasta sauce, baked or stewed, aubergine is barely discernible. Personally, I prefer them griddled, grilled or roasted as they develop a wonderfully smoky flavour and golden colour. Many people are put off aubergines by their propensity to soak up large quantities of oil during cooking. They do seem to love the stuff, but there are ways to minimize the amount of oil required. Some recipes call for salting aubergines to draw out any bitter juices and reduce their moisture content.

Although salting is not essential, it does reduce the amount of oil absorbed during cooking. If frying aubergines, don't add huge amounts of oil if they look a little dry: add a few tablespoons at first – which will be readily absorbed – then reduce the heat and cook the aubergine slowly. As they cook, the aubergines will start to release their own juices and some of the absorbed oil.

ONE PORTION
2–3 tablespoons

Maximize the nutrients

Look for firm aubergines with a glossy, smooth skin. Smaller aubergines have a slightly sweeter flavour, but a withered specimen with soft patches or wrinkles is an indication of old age and will consequently be lower in vitamins B and C, as well as iron, potassium and calcium. It has been said that the cold affects the flavour of an aubergine, so they are at their best when stored at room temperature for up to 3–5 days – they also look great in the fruit bowl.

MELTING AUBERGINE PARCELS

When the kids first spotted me making these mozzarella-stuffed aubergine slices there was a cry of "we're not eating aubergine" – hardly the response I was looking for. Thankfully the response to the finished dish was more positive! This goes well with a tomato sauce.

SERVES 4

- 1 large aubergine, peeled
- 1 ball mozzarella, sliced
- 4 vine-ripened tomatoes, thinly sliced and seeded (optional)
- plain flour, for dredging
- 2 eggs, beaten
- salt and pepper
- dried fresh breadcrumbs
- olive oil, for frying

1 Preheat the grill to medium-high and line the grill pan with foil. Cut the aubergine into 16 round slices. Blanch the slices in a little boiling water until tender, then drain well on kitchen paper.

2 Place a slice of mozzarella and 2 slices of tomato (if using) between two slices of aubergine to make a sandwich. Hold the sandwich together and dip each side into the flour, the seasoned egg and then the breadcrumbs until completely covered. Repeat with the remaining aubergine slices.

3 Heat enough oil to cover the base of a frying pan and fry the parcels for 5 minutes each side, until golden and crisp. Drain on kitchen paper before serving.

▼

HOW TO EAT MORE...

- *This Italian classic is a family favourite: make a tomato sauce (see page 102). Meanwhile, grill lightly oiled slices of aubergine until golden. Pour the tomato sauce into an ovenproof dish, top with slices of aubergine and then slices of mozzarella. Sprinkle with grated Parmesan cheese and bake in the oven for about 30–40 minutes until the cheese is golden.*
- *To make a delicious, slightly spicy dip, using a fork, prick an aubergine all over and roast it in a 200°C/400°F oven, until the middle is tender – about 35–40 minutes. Halve the aubergine lengthways and scoop the flesh into a food processor. Add a chopped clove of garlic, 1 tsp each of ground cumin and coriander, plenty of lemon juice and salt and pepper, then purée until smooth and creamy.*

Mushroom Medley

The Romans served mushrooms to their soldiers, believing they gave them enormous strength – a fact that always goes down well with boys.

One way to encourage an interest in food is to show children where it comes from. Picking wild mushrooms is good fun, but do your homework first so you know what you are looking for, arm yourself with a good mushroom guide and – obviously – be extremely careful. There's nothing more rewarding than discovering free food. Mushrooms add a meaty texture and substance to soups, stews, bakes and pies. If you find your kids balk at their texture (many find them slimy) try frying sliced mushrooms in a little olive oil and butter over a medium-high heat, tossing them frequently, until they become crisp.

In natural medicine mushrooms are revered for their healing qualities, which are believed to help fight cancer, heart disease and viral infections. In Asia, shiitake mushrooms are recommended for a long and healthy life. Mushrooms are also a useful source of selenium, potassium, iron and many of the B vitamins.

ONE PORTION
2 tablespoons

Maximize the nutrients

Since B vitamins are water-soluble, it's best not to soak or wash fresh mushrooms; they also absorb water, making them soggy. Peeling is not necessary either, simply wipe mushrooms with damp kitchen paper and trim the stems. Mushrooms will keep for up to 3 days in the fridge stored in a paper bag – plastic makes them sweat.

HOW TO EAT MORE...

- Add finely chopped mushroom to home-made burgers to keep them moist.
- Fry quartered mushrooms and a sprinkling of dried oregano in a little butter, then add a few spoonfuls of crème fraîche. Spoon onto a lightly toasted slice of bread, sprinkle with grated Cheddar cheese then grill until the cheese has melted.
- Try mushrooms baked in a foil parcel with a little butter or oil and chopped fresh tomato. Open up the parcel when the mushroom is tender and top with a slice of mozzarella. Return the parcel to the oven and cook until the cheese is melted and gooey.

GOLDEN MOONS

You can vary the type of vegetables you use in these pasties, depending on what you have to hand. You will have some of the filling left over, but this can be frozen for later use.

2-3

MAKES 8 PASTIES

- 1 tbsp olive oil
- 1 large onion, finely chopped
- 200 g/7 oz lean mince or vegetarian alternative
- 1 large clove garlic, finely chopped
- 1 tsp dried thyme
- 1 large carrot, grated
- 100 g/3½ oz brown cap mushrooms, very finely chopped
- 55 g/2 oz white cabbage, grated
- 2 tsp Worcestershire sauce
- 1 tsp Dijon mustard
- 1 tbsp tomato purée
- 250 ml/9 fl oz canned

chopped tomatoes
- salt and pepper
- 500 g/1 lb 2 oz pack ready-made puff pastry, defrosted
- flour, for dusting
- 1 egg beaten, for glazing

1 Heat the oil in a heavy-based saucepan and fry the onion for 8 minutes, until softened. Add the mince, stirring to break up the meat, until browned. (If using vegetarian mince, add it after the cabbage.) Add the garlic, thyme, carrot, mushrooms and cabbage and cook, stirring, for 5 minutes.

2 Preheat the oven to 200°C/400°F. Stir in the Worcestershire sauce, mustard, tomato purée and tomatoes, season, and bring to the boil. Reduce the heat and simmer for 10 minutes until the sauce has reduced and thickened. Leave to cool.

3 Roll out the pastry on a floured surface and cut into 8 13 cm (5 in) squares. Brush the edges with beaten egg, then place a spoonful of the filling on one half of the square, leaving a space around the edge. Fold the pastry over to encase the filling and to make a triangle. Press the edges with a fork to seal and fold back the corners to make a crescent. Prick the top with a fork and brush with egg.

4 Place the pasties on a lightly greased baking sheet and bake for 18–20 minutes until golden.

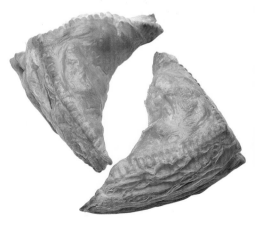

Pukka Peppers

With their juicy flesh, crisp texture and vibrant colour, sweet peppers are perfect served raw. Slice them into strips or try using a pastry cutter to make different shapes. Any food that does not require a knife and fork to eat always goes down well, and a dip served with a plateful of vegetable sticks that includes peppers allows kids to help themselves and gives them some power over their food choices.

ONE PORTION
2–3 tablespoons

Red peppers have a sweeter flavour than green, because peppers change from green through to yellow, orange and red as they ripen. Green peppers are fully developed but not completely ripe, which accounts for their slightly bitter flavour and is the reason why some people find them difficult to digest.

Peppers are a major source of vitamin C – a green pepper provides twice as much vitamin C weight for weight than an orange, while red peppers contain three times as much! Peppers are also rich in beta-carotene – red peppers providing nine times as much as green.

HOW TO EAT MORE...

- *Halve a red or orange pepper lengthways and scoop out the seeds. Place in an oiled baking dish and fill each half with a bean stew or bolognese sauce. Cover the dish with foil and bake in a 200°C/400°F oven for about 35 minutes. Remove the foil, sprinkle with grated Cheddar cheese and cook for 5 more minutes.*
- *Roast chunks of red pepper and butternut squash with wedges of red onion for about 35 minutes. Leave to cool slightly then purée until smooth. Serve stirred into mashed potato.*

Maximize the nutrients

Since vitamin C is partially destroyed by heat, it is better to eat peppers raw. But if you are cooking them, try roasting, stir-frying or chargrilling rather than steaming or boiling them. The bioavailability of beta-carotene, however, is increased by lightly cooking peppers in a dish that contains a little olive oil or similar monounsaturated fat. Always look for firm, unwrinkled, glossy skinned peppers with no sign of discoloration.

MAGIC STICKS

These delicious vegetable kebabs are equally good baked, grilled or barbecued. Serve with vegetable crudités and roasted new potatoes.

MAKES 16

- 1 frozen garlic bread baton
- 1 large red pepper, seeded and cut into 16 large pieces
- 16 cherry tomatoes
- 250 g/9 oz halloumi cheese, cut into 8 slices, then each slice halved
- olive oil, for brushing

1 Preheat the oven to 200°C/400°F. Soak 16 wooden skewers in water for 30 minutes to prevent them from burning. Partially defrost the garlic bread until barely soft enough to cut. Slice into 8, then cut each round in half to make 16 pieces.

2 Thread a piece of garlic bread onto each wooden skewer, followed by a cherry tomato, a piece of cheese (take care, it is quite fragile) then a chunk of pepper.

3 Place the skewers on a lightly oiled baking sheet. Brush the pepper, tomatoes and edges of the bread with a little olive oil. Cover with foil and cook for 5 minutes. Remove the foil, turning over the kebabs and cook for another 5 minutes until the pepper and tomatoes are cooked and the bread is crisp.

Sunny Sweetcorn

Its sweet tender kernels makes sweetcorn a natural favourite. And munching on a warm corn-on-the-cob with butter running down the fingers is very appealing! Corn-on-the-cob is best eaten soon after picking, before the natural sugars start to convert into starch, when the flavour fades and the kernels toughen. If you can, buy locally grown corn in season, with the green outer leaves intact. Remove the leaves before steaming. The cob is ready when a kernel can be easily pulled out. Barbecuing or roasting enhances the corn's sweetness, but it's best to blanch cobs for a couple of minutes first to soften the kernels.

ONE PORTION
2–3 tablespoons

Canned corn is a great store cupboard standby, although it is lower in nutrients than fresh corn. Choose the no-added sugar and salt variety, and drain and rinse before use.

Rich in complex carbohydrates, sweetcorn is a good source of vitamins A, B and C as well as fibre. It also contains useful amounts of potassium, iron, magnesium and folate.

Maximize the nutrients

Water-soluble B vitamins are lost during boiling, so sweetcorn is best steamed or microwaved until just tender. Canned corn is a good source of readily usable fibre, although frozen corn tends to be a better source of nutrients. Nutrients are at their optimum when the fresh kernels are plump and show no signs of wrinkling or discoloration. Eat soon after purchase, but if you don't intend to use them straight away, you can store the cobs in the fridge for a few days.

HOW TO EAT MORE...

- *Blanch a corn-on-cob for 5 minutes in boiling water until just tender. Drain, then add a little butter and 1 tsp honey to the pan. Return the cob to the pan and cook for 4 minutes, turning the cob occasionally, until glossy and golden. Alternatively, barbecue or griddle after coating in butter and honey.*
- *To make sweetcorn fritters: using a pestle and mortar, crush 225 g/8 oz sweetcorn. Fry 1 small chopped onion until golden, then leave to cool. Combine the corn and onion with 1 egg and 2 tbsp of plain flour, season. Heat some oil in a frying pan and drop a large tablespoonful of the batter into the hot oil. Fry for about 3 minutes on each side until golden.*

SWEETCORN & SMOKED HADDOCK CHOWDER

The sweetcorn adds creaminess to this satisfying soup. In this recipe, I blend the vegetables until smooth, just leaving chunks of fish. But you could half-purée the vegetables so you still have some chunks. It is served in a hollowed-out loaf in traditional San Francisco-style.

SERVES 4

- 1 tbsp sunflower oil
- 1 large leek, sliced
- 1 large red pepper, seeded and chopped
- 1 stick celery, sliced
- 1 carrot, sliced
- 2 potatoes, peeled and cubed
- 1 bay leaf
- 850 ml/1½ pts vegetable stock
- 400 g/14 oz can no-sugar or salt sweetcorn, drained and rinsed, or equivalent amount fresh or frozen
- 500 g/1 lb 2 oz undyed smoked haddock fillet

- 250 ml/9 fl oz milk
- 2 tbsp crème fraîche or single cream
- salt and pepper
- 4 small round loaves or large rolls

1 Heat the oil in a large saucepan and fry the leek over a medium heat for 5 minutes, until softened. Add the red pepper, celery, carrot, potatoes and bay leaf and cook, stirring, for a further 5 minutes.

2 Pour in the stock, bring to the boil and reduce the heat. Half-cover the pan and cook for 20 minutes, adding the sweetcorn in the final 5 minutes.

3 Meanwhile, put the haddock in a large shallow pan and cover with water. Bring to the boil then simmer for about 6–8 minutes, until just cooked and opaque. Carefully remove the fish from the pan and leave until cool enough to handle. Peel off the skin, remove any bones, and flake the fish into large chunks.

4 Pour the soup into a blender or use a hand-held blender to half-purée or completely purée until fairly smooth. Return the soup to the pan and stir in the milk, crème fraîche and fish, season well, then warm through.

5 To serve, slice the top off each loaf to make a lid and hollow out the insides of the loaf – keeping the bread either for dunking in the soup or to dry to make breadcrumbs. Pour the soup into the hollowed-out loaves and top with the lid.

Top Tomatoes

Children either love or loathe tomatoes, but when I talk to parents about how they get their kids to eat more vegetables, tomato sauce (and I don't mean ketchup) is a popular reply. A real tomato sauce is the perfect foil for hiding various vegetables. Finely chop carrot, courgette, onion or red pepper, and sauté them in oil before adding to the tomatoes. Purée in a food processor for a smooth sauce or alternatively steam the vegetables first, purée in a blender then stir into the almost-cooked sauce. Try adding canned pulses such as chickpeas to further boost the nutritional content, or add a spoonful of humous or cream cheese for a delicious creaminess.

If your kids prefer their tomatoes raw, try all the different types – from cute cherry tomatoes to large beefsteaks (also perfect for stuffing).

Tomatoes are a good source of beta-carotene and vitamins C and E as well as flavonoids and lycopene, which has been shown to be effective in reducing the risk of heart disease and cancer.

ONE PORTION
1 medium-sized tomato

Maximize the nutrients

Buy tomatoes in small amounts and eat when ripe for maximum nutritional benefits. Ideally, keep tomatoes at room temperature, not in the fridge as this spoils their flavour. Vine-ripened tomatoes contain more vitamin C than those picked when they are still green.

Lycopene is best absorbed when tomatoes are cooked and in a concentrated form such as in a sauce, paste or soup. Absorption of beta-carotene is enhanced by heat and oil. Vitamin C is mainly found in the jelly-like coating around tomato seeds.

HOW TO EAT MORE...

- *For a quick tomato sauce, fry a chopped clove of garlic in olive oil and add a can of chopped plum tomatoes, 1 tbsp tomato purée and a pinch of sugar. Cook for 10–15 minutes.*
- *For a quick breakfast, take a slice of bread and toast one side. Top the untoasted side with a chopped fresh tomato then sprinkle with grated cheese. Grill until golden.*
- *For a quick pizza, halve a wholemeal muffin and top with a large spoonful of tomato sauce. Sprinkle over mozzarella or Cheddar cheese and grill until melted.*

ALL-IN-ONE TUNA RISOTTO

Risottos can be time consuming to prepare, but this version couldn't be simpler. All you do is put the ingredients in an ovenproof dish and bung it in the oven! Serve with steamed broccoli.

SERVES 4

- 1 tbsp olive oil
- 25 g/1 oz butter
- 1 large onion, finely chopped
- 2 cloves garlic, chopped
- 1–2 tsp dried oregano
- 300 g/10½ oz risotto rice
- 1 glass of dry white wine
- 500 ml/18 fl oz passata
- 500 ml/18 fl oz vegetable stock
- 300 g/10½ oz canned tuna in olive oil, drained
- 85 g/3 oz frozen peas
- salt and pepper

1 Pre-heat the oven to 180°C/350°F. Heat the oil and butter in a large ovenproof saucepan. Add the onion and fry over a medium heat for about 8 minutes, until softened. Add the garlic and oregano and cook for another minute. Stir in the rice and cook for a few minutes.

2 Pour in the wine, then bring to the boil and cook until it has evaporated and there is no smell of alcohol. Now add the passata and stock. Give it a good stir, cover, and place in the oven for 15 minutes.

3 Remove from the oven and stir in the tuna and peas and cook for another 5–10 minutes until the rice is plump and tender. Season to taste.

Salad Days

There is such a wide selection of leaves to choose from that you're bound to find something your child likes. Adopt a theme for your salads and vary the ingredients accordingly: a country garden salad, a picnic salad, a seaside salad (see right), or a summer salad – all using seasonal ingredients. Cress appeals to children and can be easily grown at home in an egg box containing damp cotton wool or tissue. Rocket and different varieties of lettuce can be grown in a pot or window box.

Dressings make all the difference to the success of a salad. Experiment with different types of oils and vinegars. I've found the sweetness of balsamic vinegar is a favourite, while creamy dressings take the edge off bitter flavours. It's worth remembering that lettuce leaves are said to have a calming, sedative effect, so a bowlful may be beneficial at teatime!

ONE PORTION
1 dessert-bowlful

Maximize the nutrients

The outer darker leaves of a lettuce contain a higher ratio of folate, beta-carotene, vitamin C, calcium and iron than the paler leaves found in the centre. The nutritional value can also vary depending on the time of year and the freshness of the leaves. Lettuce can be high in nitrates and pesticides, so wash leaves thoroughly but gently to avoid damaging them (better still, choose organic), and tear rather than cut them to preserve the nutrients. The oil used in the dressing will increase the availability of the beta-carotene in the leaves.

HOW TO EAT MORE...

- Large crisp lettuce leaves can be used as a wrap: fill with a noodle salad, rice salad or a selection of roasted vegetables, pesto and mozzarella.
- Combine shredded spinach and Cos lettuce with quartered hard-boiled egg, crispy bacon and tomato wedges to make a main meal.
- Make a colourful salad platter by arranging Little Gem lettuce leaves, pepper, celery and carrot sticks, sliced cucumber, halved cherry tomatoes, sweetcorn, olives, cubes of cooked beetroot and canned beans on a large serving plate. Place three different salad dressings in bowls and let your children make up their own mixed salad and help themselves to the dressings.
- Transform watercress, lettuce or spinach into a delicious soup.

SEASIDE SALAD

Use pasta shells to give a seaside feel to this prawn salad. You can use brain-boosting canned salmon, mackerel or tuna instead of prawns. If making this salad for a lunch box, make sure it can be refrigerated, if not, omit the seafood.

SERVES 4

- 150 g/5½ oz pasta shells
- 140 g/5 oz cooked prawns or canned salmon, mackerel or tuna
- 8 cherry tomatoes, halved
- 1 red pepper, seeded and diced
- 2 spring onions, finely chopped
- 4 large crisp iceberg lettuce leaves and watercress, to serve

For the dressing:
- 4 tbsp mayonnaise
- 1 tbsp olive oil
- 2 tbsp tomato ketchup
- salt and pepper

1 Cook the pasta in plenty of boiling salted water, following the packet instructions. Drain well, transfer to a large bowl and toss the pasta in a little olive oil. Leave to cool slightly.

2 Mix together the ingredients for the dressing and season to taste.

3 Add the prawns (or other fish), tomatoes, pepper and spring onions to the pasta and spoon over the dressing. Toss until the salad is coated.

4 Place the iceberg lettuce leaves on serving plates and top with the watercress. Spoon over the pasta salad and serve.

BEANS,
SPROUTS &
PULSES

Alfalfa For Ever!

Unusual in that it is one of the few plant foods that is a complete protein, alfalfa contains all eight essential amino acids, which are crucial for maintenance and growth. Alfalfa sprouts are reputed to have the ability to rejuvenate and cleanse the body and aid digestion. They are also a wonderful source of vitamins and minerals, providing calcium, phosphorus, potassium and iron as well as vitamins A, B and C.

The sprouting process enhances the nutrients already found in the seeds and boosts their enzyme content. Plant enzymes boost metabolism and are good for the skin, stress and fatigue.

ONE PORTION
A handful

Maximize the nutrients

The leaves, seeds and sprouts of alfalfa are all edible. You can buy ready-sprouted alfalfa in health food stores and some supermarkets, but look for healthy crisp sprouts and make sure there is no sign of mushiness or decay. The slender, nutritious sprouts are cheap to buy but make sure you get them from a reliable source. Alfalfa is most nutritious when eaten raw and, conveniently, doesn't need cleaning or any preparation before use.

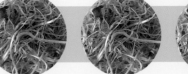

GROW-YOUR-OWN ALFALFA

Alfalfa is incredibly easy to grow at home and, if you get kids involved in the growing, it's that much easier to get them eating. It only takes a few days to grow, but you will have to rinse the sprouts about four times a day to ensure healthy growth. Make sure the seeds have not been treated with fungicides.

You will need
- Alfalfa seeds
- Large glass jar
- Small piece of muslin
- Rubber band

1 Pick over the seeds to remove any damaged ones, then soak in plenty of tepid water for up to 12 hours. Drain well, then put the seeds in a clean, sterilized jar.

2 Place a small piece of muslin over the top of the jar and secure with a rubber band. Stand in a warm, light place.

3 Rinse the seeds in the jar under cold running water, then drain them well — try not to disturb the seeds too much. You will need to rinse them a minimum of twice a day, preferably four times a day.

4 The sprouts will be ready in 3–5 days; the seeds should have a slender white stem and small green leaves. If the weather is cold, the seeds will take slightly longer to grow.

5 Transfer the sprouts to an airtight container and store for up to one week in the refrigerator.

HOW TO EAT MORE...
- *Sprinkle alfalfa over salads or in sandwiches or wraps.*
- *Mix in a handful of alfalfa with home-made meat or vegetarian burgers.*
- *Add to stir-fries, soups, stews, and bakes.*
- *Combine a handful in paté or dip recipes.*
- *Sprinkle the unsprouted seeds into bread dough or pastry to give a pleasant nutty crunch.*
- *To make "egg-in-a-nest" salad, take an iceberg lettuce leaf and top with a handful of alfalfa sprouts. Hard boil an egg, shell and cut in half. Place the egg in the lettuce and alfalfa nest and top with a spoonful of mayonnaise.*

Bursting Bean Sprouts

We're all familiar with mung bean sprouts, the long translucent white shoots with a crunchy texture and delicate flavour. Yet chickpeas, lentils, aduki and soya beans are also good for sprouting. You can buy mixed bags of ready-sprouted beans in most health food shops but if you want to have a go yourself, beans are easy and cheap to sprout at home. Follow the instructions for alfalfa (see page 109) but soak the beans overnight beforehand. Make sure you gently rinse them 2–4 times a day. They will be ready to eat in 4–6 days. If adding bean sprouts to a stir-fry, scatter a handful towards the end of cooking to preserve their crispness as well as the nutrients which diminish when cooked.

Unlike most fruits and vegetables which begin to lose their nutrient content as soon as they are picked, bean sprouts continue to increase their concentration of vitamins and minerals when sprouted. There is around 30 percent more B vitamins and 60 percent more vitamin C in the sprout than in the bean when it's in its natural state; a single portion provides almost 100 percent of the recommended daily amount of vitamin C.

ONE PORTION
A handful or 2–3 heaped tablespoons

HOW TO EAT MORE...

- Mung beans, chick peas and soya beans produce sizeable sprouts that can be eaten as a snack on their own.
- Sprinkle a handful in sandwiches, pitta bread or wraps to boost their nutritional content. Humous, guacamole, grated cheese or boiled egg are good accompaniments.
- Use soya, chickpea or lentil sprouts in stews and bakes.
- Sprouted aduki beans can be added to burger, meatloaf or rissole mixes.
- Add crunch to salads with a handful of sprouted beans. They work best with other crisp salad ingredients such as Chinese leaves, sweet pepper, carrot and onion.

Maximize the nutrients

Look for fresh crisp bean sprouts, ideally with the bean still attached, with no sign of mushiness or decay. If sprouting your own, store them an airtight container in the refrigerator – they will last up to 5 days. Bean sprouts are most nutritious when eaten raw and don't need any preparation before use.

SPRING ROLLS WITH DIPPING SAUCE

Children can help to make these crispy spring rolls filled with vegetables and noodles. I've baked them in the oven to keep fat levels down but you can fry them.

MAKES 20

- 70 g/2½ oz vermicelli noodles
- 2 tsp vegetable oil, plus extra for brushing
- 1 tsp toasted sesame oil
- 2 carrots, cut into thin strips
- 1 red pepper, cut into thin strips
- 2 spring onions, finely sliced lengthways
- 100 g/3½ oz mange tout, thinly sliced on the diagonal
- 2.5 cm/1 in piece fresh root ginger, peeled and grated
- 1 tbsp soy sauce
- 100 g/3½ oz beansprouts
- 20 small spring roll wrappers, defrosted

- 1 egg white, lightly beaten

For the dipping sauce:
- 4 tbsp sweet plum sauce
- 1 tbsp soy sauce

1 Soak the noodles in just boiled water as instructed on the packet. Drain, then refresh under cold running water. Cut the noodles into short lengths.

2 Heat the oils in a wok. Add the carrots, pepper, spring onions and mange tout and stir-fry for 3 minutes, tossing continuously. Add the ginger, soy sauce and bean sprouts and cook for another minute until the liquid evaporates. Transfer the vegetables into a bowl with the noodles and mix until combined; leave to cool.

3 Preheat the oven to 180°C/ 350°F. Place a spring roll wrapper on a work surface, keeping the rest covered with a tea towel to prevent them drying out. Place a heaped tbsp of the filling on the corner nearest you, then fold the corner over the filling towards the centre. Fold in the two sides of the wrapper to enclose the filling, then continue to roll. Brush the far corner with a little egg white and fold over to seal. Repeat to make 20 rolls.

4 Lightly brush a large baking sheet with oil. Arrange the spring rolls on the sheet and brush each one with oil. Bake in the oven for 15–20 minutes until lightly golden and crisp on the outside.

5 To make the dipping sauce, mix together the plum sauce and soy sauce in a small bowl and serve with the spring rolls.

Lively Lentils

The humble lentil's unassuming flavour and soft texture means that it gladly takes on stronger flavours and can be transformed into all manner of child-friendly dishes, from burgers to soups. In India, lentils are used in spicy dahls or lentil curries, whereas in the Middle East, red or yellow lentils are mixed with spices and vegetables to form balls known as kofte, similar to falafel. Unlike pulses, lentils don't require pre-soaking and take less time to cook, with the red split lentil taking less than 20 minutes, eventually disintegrating into a thick purée. Ideal for thickening and adding substance to soups and casseroles, a handful of cooked red lentils in a tomato sauce will give a boost to its nutritional value.

Green and brown lentils can be blended with herbs or spices to make a tasty pâté, and puy lentils are great in hearty rustic dishes.

They take marginally longer to cook, but after cooking they can be stored in the fridge for a few days or frozen for later use.

Lentils provide an impressive range of nutrients including iron, zinc, folate, manganese, selenium, phosphorus and some B vitamins. Low in fat and higher in protein than most pulses, lentils are also an excellent source of fibre.

ONE PORTION
2–3 tablespoons

HOW TO EAT MORE...

- Cook lentils in vegetable stock (following packet instructions) until tender. Drain well and combine with fried onion, garlic, celery, carrot and a splash of soy sauce. Blend to make a paté or spread.
- Add cooked puy lentils to a salad incorporating flakes of tuna, Cos lettuce, diced tomato, spring onion and red pepper. Pour over a lemony vinaigrette dressing.
- Add cooked red split lentils to roasts, burgers or rissoles in place of – or as well as – nuts, beans or meat.

Maximize the nutrients

Cook lentils in the minimum amount of water to maximize their vitamin B content, or cook as part of a stew or soup. If you eat lentils with foods that are rich in vitamin C, such as tomatoes, you will absorb a greater amount of their iron content.

SPICY LENTIL & CARROT SOUP

Hearty and filling, this nutritious soup uses a Moroccan spice paste but you could try an Indian blend, such as garam masala, instead. Either way, the spicing is quite subtle.

3

SERVES 4

- 1 tbsp olive oil
- 1 large onion, chopped
- 1 stick celery, with leaves, chopped
- 300 g/10½ oz carrots, sliced
- 175 g/6 oz red split lentils
- 1 tsp ground coriander
- 1 tsp ground cumin
- 1 tsp turmeric
- 4 tomatoes, seeded and chopped
- 1.2 litres/2 pints vegetable stock
- 1 heaped tsp Moroccan tagine paste
- salt and pepper

For the garlic croutons:
- 2 slices day-old wholemeal bread, crusts removed
- 2 cloves garlic, peeled and halved lengthways
- 1–2 tbsp olive oil

1 Heat the olive oil in a large saucepan and fry the onion for 8 minutes over a medium heat until softened. Add the celery and carrots and cook, stirring frequently, for another 3 minutes. Stir in the lentils and spices and cook for a further minute.

2 Add the tomatoes and stock, then bring to the boil, skimming off any foam from the lentils that rises to the surface. Reduce the heat, mix in the tagine paste, then half cover the pan and simmer for about 20 minutes. Stir regularly to prevent the lentils sticking to the bottom of the pan.

3 Transfer the soup to a blender or use a hand-held blender and process until smooth. Season to taste and reheat the soup if necessary.

4 To make the croutons, rub both sides of each slice of bread with the garlic. Cut the bread into cubes and place in a small plastic bag with the olive oil. Shake to coat the bread in the oil, then fry in a heavy-based frying pan until golden and crisp. Sprinkle over the soup just before serving.

Punchy Pulses

The term "pulses" includes beans and peas from a very large family of plants, the *leguminosae*, one of which is the haricot bean, used to make baked beans – and, I'm happy to say, baked beans count in the five-a-day guidelines! Most kids go through a baked beans phase and it can't be denied that they are an incredibly convenient addition to the store cupboard. The low-salt, low-sugar variety is now widely available – and although they take some getting use to, their health benefits make them definitely preferable.

Don't forget all the other types of pulses, for these edible seeds of plants have many health benefits, providing plenty of slow-release energy thanks to a combination of carbohydrate, protein and soluble fibre – and all in a low-fat form.

They are very filling: a meal containing pulses will satisfy the appetite for longer than most other foods – a definite asset, especially for those parents with children who are constant "snackers". There are many different types of pulses to choose from and their ability to add substance and absorb the flavours of other foods means that pulses are infinitely versatile. Use them in home-made burgers, vegetable or meat loaves, pies, stews, soups, dips, salads, curries, pasta sauces, combined

ONE PORTION
2–3 heaped tablespoons

with rice and more. However, it's worth remembering that pulses only count as a single portion in the five-a-day guidelines, however much you eat in a day.

Dried pulses are inexpensive but do require forward planning, since most pulses need prolonged soaking and lengthy cooking. If you can't be doing with this – and who can? – canned pulses make an excellent alternative. Modern canning methods mean that canned pulses are often more nutritious than fresh or dried, especially if they have been hanging around for a while. The fibre in canned pulses is also more readily absorbed by the body. But do take care when giving high-fibre foods to babies and young children, as they can find them difficult to digest in large quantities – too much can lead to stomach upsets and loss of appetite.

Canned pulses tend to be softer than cooked dried pulses, so only require heating through. They are easy to mash, which means they're good for child-friendly dishes such as burgers, rissoles, bean and potato mash, stuffings and dips. However, try to avoid canned pulses that contain added salt and sometimes sugar, usually labelled "in brine". If these are the only ones available, make sure you drain and rinse them before use.

Pulses are rich in iron, potassium, phosphorus, folate, magnesium, manganese and most B vitamins. They also contain a concentration of phytochemicals including lignins, known for their heart-protective and anti-cancer benefits.

Maximize the nutrients

A recent survey carried out by the UK Canned Food Association found that canned kidney beans contain double the calcium of the same serving of dried, cooked kidney beans, while canned chickpeas are similar to fresh, but provide around 35 per cent more vitamin E. Acid foods such as tomatoes, vinegar or lemon juice toughen dried pulses (as does salt) during cooking, making them more difficult to digest. It is best to add these once the pulses have softened, or alternatively use canned pulses.

It is now possible to buy some pulses in their fresh form, but do make sure they are as fresh and young as possible to avoid a loss of nutrients. It is best to buy dried pulses in small quantities from shops with a regular turnover of stock. The older they are, the drier they become and the lower their nutritional content. Avoid dried pulses that look dusty and dirty. Pulses are best stored in an airtight container in a cool, dark, dry place.

▼

HOW TO EAT MORE...

- *Add canned or cooked dried beans to shop-bought or home-made soups.*
- *Add puréed or mashed cannellini beans, butter beans or lima beans to boost the nutritional content of mashed potatoes.*
- *Add baked beans to a sausage hotpot or vegetable stew.*
- *Make your own low-salt and sugar baked beans by mixing together 1 tbsp olive oil, 200 g/7 oz can drained and rinsed haricot beans, 150 ml/5 fl oz passata, 1 tsp Dijon mustard, 1 tbsp each of Worcestershire sauce, maple syrup and tomato purée in a saucepan. Bring to the boil, then simmer, half-covered, for 15–20 minutes until the sauce has reduced and thickened.*
- *Chickpeas help to bulk out curries and dishes made with noodles.*
- *Stir chopped raw tomatoes into canned baked beans.*

What to choose

Here is a round-up of the most readily available pulses and tips on how to use them.

- **Aduki beans** are tiny red or yellow beans that have a sweet, nutty flavour. They are popular in Chinese cooking, where they are turned into a red bean paste, but can also be added to stews and bakes. They are higher in zinc than other pulses and are also good when sprouted.
- **Cannellini beans** are kidney-shaped beans and have a soft, creamy texture and slightly firm outer skin. Use in place of haricot beans in stews, purées or dips.
- **Borlotti beans** are oval shaped and have a pinky-brown skin and slightly sweet flavour. They work well in stews or soups.
- **Broad or fava beans** are usually bought fresh or frozen. The outer skin can be very tough, so it is best to peel them after cooking.
- **Flageolet beans** are small, mint-green beans, with a delicate flavour that appeals to children. They are great in salads, dips and purées.
- **Chickpeas** have a slightly nutty flavour and texture. They are used in Mediterranean and Middle Eastern cooking.

- **Black beans** are shiny kidney-shaped beans that are often used in Caribbean dishes such as stews and soups.
- **Black-eyed beans** (peas) are often used in Creole and Indian cooking. The creamy coloured beans have a characteristic black spot on the side and are great in curries, soups and bakes.
- **Butter beans** and **lima beans** are similar in appearance and flavour. The flattish, kidney-shaped beans have a soft, floury texture when cooked making them ideal puréed or mashed in soups and stews.
- **Haricot beans** are used to make canned baked beans. Ivory-coloured and oval in shape, they are most suited to slow-cooked dishes such as stews and bakes.
- **Pinto beans** are a smaller version of the borlotti bean and are known as the "painted bean" due to their speckled skin. Combined with garlic, chilli, tomatoes and oil then mashed to make a rough purée and served with warm tortillas, they are best-known in Mexican refried beans.
- **Red kidney beans** retain their shape and colour when cooked and are used to make spicy chillies as well as refried beans. They also make a colourful addition to salads.

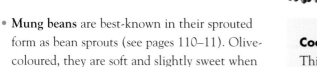

- **Mung beans** are best-known in their sprouted form as bean sprouts (see pages 110–11). Olive-coloured, they are soft and slightly sweet when cooked and are especially good in curries.
- **Soya beans** are super-healthy, being one of the very few plant foods that is a complete protein (see pages 122–5).

How to prepare & cook dried pulses

It's debatable whether soaking dried pulses before cooking is necessary. It does, however, help to reduce cooking times and make them more digestible. Rinse the pulses in a sieve placed under a cold running tap, then place them in a bowl and cover with fresh cold water. Leave to soak overnight. There is a fast method of soaking, especially useful if you've forgotten to plan in advance. After rinsing, place the pulses in a pan, cover with cold water, bring to the boil and cook for 3 minutes. Remove from the heat and leave to stand, covered, for 45–60 minutes. Rinse the pulses again, then put them back in the pan, cover with more fresh water and bring to the boil. Boil rapidly for 10–15 minutes (the latter for red kidney beans) then reduce the heat and simmer until tender (see cooking times chart). Do not add salt to the cooking water as it will toughen the beans.

Cooking times for dried pulses

This is a general guide, as cooking times vary depending on the age of the pulses.

Aduki beans	30–45 minutes
Black beans	1 hour
Black-eyed beans	45–60 minutes
Borlotti beans	1–1½ hours
Broad beans	1½ hours
Butter/lima beans	1–1¼ hours
Cannellini beans	1 hour
Chickpeas	1½–2 hours
Flageolet beans	1½ hours
Haricot beans	1–1½ hours
Kidney beans	1–1½ hours
Mung beans	25–40 minutes
Pinto beans	1–1¼ hours
Soya beans	2–3 hours

MEXICAN BEAN TACOS

Tacos are the perfect container for meat, vegetable and bean-based stews. Serve the tacos with cucumber and pepper sticks and some shredded lettuce.

SERVES 4

- 1 tbsp olive oil
- 1 large onion, finely chopped
- 1 stick celery, finely chopped
- 1 large red pepper, seeded and diced
- 1 large carrot, finely grated
- 1 large clove garlic, crushed
- 1 tsp dried oregano
- ½ tsp paprika
- 1 tsp ground coriander
- 400 g/14 oz can chopped tomatoes
- 400 g/14 oz can no-salt or sugar red kidney beans, drained and rinsed
- 75 ml/2½ fl oz vegetable stock
- salt and pepper

To serve:
- 6–8 tacos
- grated cheese
- soured cream or guacamole

1 Heat the oil in a heavy-based saucepan and fry the onion for 8 minutes, until softened. Add the celery, red pepper, carrot, garlic, oregano and spices and cook for another 6 minutes, stirring frequently.

2 Add the tomatoes, kidney beans and stock and bring to a boil. Reduce the heat and simmer for 10–15 minutes, until the sauce has reduced and thickened; you can add some water if it seems too dry.

3 Warm the tacos, spoon in the stew, sprinkle with cheese and add a spoonful of soured cream or guacamole before serving.

BROAD BEAN FALAFEL

Perfect for lunch boxes, these mixed bean falafels are equally good served hot or cold. The mini pittas are a convenient size for children and will hold a couple of falafel each. I've suggested some accompaniments that will boost the vegetable count.

SERVES 4

- 140 g/5 oz shelled broad beans, fresh or frozen
- 125 g/4½ oz (drained weight) canned chickpeas, rinsed
- 2 cloves garlic, crushed
- 2 spring onions, finely sliced
- 1 tsp ground cumin
- 1 tsp ground coriander
- 1 tsp lemon juice
- 1 tbsp fresh mint, chopped
- 1 tbsp fresh parsley, chopped
- 1 free-range egg, beaten
- salt and pepper
- flour, for dusting
- sunflower oil, for frying

To serve:
- mini pitta bread
- guacamole
- sliced Little Gem lettuce
- sliced tomato

1 Steam the broad beans for 2 minutes, then refresh under cold running water until cool.

2 Pop the beans out of their tough outer shell and put them in a food processor with the chickpeas, garlic, spring onions, spices, lemon juice, herbs and egg. Season well and blend until the mixture forms a coarse paste. Chill for 1 hour to allow the mixture to firm up.

3 Using floured hands, form the mixture into 12 walnut-size balls, then roll in flour until lightly coated. Shake to remove any excess flour.

4 Heat 1 tbsp oil in a frying pan and cook the falafels in batches (adding more oil if necessary) for 6 minutes, turning occasionally, until golden. Drain on kitchen paper and serve 2 falafels in each pitta, with a spoon of guacamole and some sliced tomato and lettuce.

Punchy Pulses

NUTTY CHICKPEA BURGERS

These burgers couldn't be easier to make and are a nutritious combination of beans, vegetables and nuts. Serve in a seeded wholemeal bun, spread with humous and sliced tomato, lettuce and alfalfa sprouts.

MAKES 6

- 400 g/14 oz can no-salt or sugar chickpeas, drained and rinsed
- 1 large onion, grated
- 2 cloves garlic, crushed
- 1 carrot, finely grated
- ½ tsp English mustard powder
- 2 tbsp peanut butter
- 100 g/3½ oz unsalted roasted cashew nuts
- 1 slice wholemeal bread
- 1 egg, beaten
- salt and pepper
- flour, for dusting
- 2 tbsp sunflower oil, for frying

1 Put all the ingredients, except the flour and oil, in a food processor and blend to a coarse purée. Chill the mixture for 30 minutes.

2 Using floured hands, divide the mixture into 6 burgers then lightly dust them with flour until coated. Brush off any excess flour.

3 Heat the oil in a heavy-based frying pan and cook the burgers0in two batches (adding more oil if necessary) for 4 minutes each side, until golden.

DIPS & DIPPERS

Children love finger food and these fun, nutritious and filling dips and dippers make a popular light lunch or tea, or can be served as party fare. To add to the appeal, you can serve the dips in hollowed out rolls, and stick the dippers on cocktail sticks into the outside of the rolls to resemble hedgehogs.

SERVES 10

Cannellini bean dip

- 2 tbsp olive oil
- 2 cloves garlic, crushed
- 400 g/14 oz can no-salt or sugar cannellini beans, drained and rinsed
- juice of ½–1 lemon, to taste
- 1 tsp dried oregano
- 2 tbsp water
- salt and pepper

1 Heat the oil in a saucepan and fry the garlic for 1 minute. Add the beans, lemon juice, oregano and water, then heat through, stirring continuously.

2 Transfer the bean mixture to a food processor and blend until smooth. Season and serve warm or cold.

Red pepper humous

- 1 large red pepper, seeded and quartered
- 4 tbsp extra-virgin olive oil
- 400 g/14 oz can no-salt or sugar chickpeas, drained and rinsed
- 2 cloves garlic, crushed
- 2 tbsp light tahini
- 2 tbsp warm water
- juice of 1 lemon
- salt and pepper

1 Preheat the oven to 200°C/400°F. Place the pepper in a roasting dish with a tbsp of the oil. Roast the pepper for 30 minutes until tender and the skin begins to blister. Place in a plastic bag, leave to cool slightly, then peel off the skin.

2 Place the pepper, chickpeas, garlic, tahini, water, lemon juice and the rest of the oil in a food processor or blender and purée until smooth. Season to taste.

Bean & avocado dip

- 200 g/7 oz can no-salt or sugar flageolet beans, drained and rinsed
- 1 avocado, stoned and flesh scooped out
- 1 small cucumber, peeled and cut into small chunks
- 2 cloves garlic, crushed
- 200 ml/7 fl oz milk
- juice of 1–2 limes, to taste
- 4 tbsp mint
- 2 tbsp extra-virgin olive oil
- salt and pepper

1 Put the beans, avocado, cucumber, garlic, milk, juice of 1 lime, mint and oil in a blender. Process until smooth.

2 Taste and add more lime juice if preferred, then season. Blend again if you add more lime.

Satisfying Soya Beans

The "superheroes" of the bean world, soya beans are the most nutritious of all pulses. Known as the "meat of the earth" in China, they are one of the few plant foods to be a complete protein, which means they contain all the essential amino acids (protein building blocks); a quality normally reserved for animal-derived foods such as meat, fish, eggs and dairy products.

The small oval beans, which vary in colour from creamy-yellow through brown to black, are best in highly flavoured dishes that include garlic, herbs or spices, such as curries, stews, Oriental dishes and hearty soups. They can also be sprouted and added to salads and stir-fries, while an ideal addition to lunchboxes are the crunchy flavoured soya bean snacks, sold in health food shops as a healthy alternative to crisps.

Yet there is more to soya than just beans. Tofu (soya bean curd) is made in much the same way as soft cheese and although it's not officially on the list of what counts in the five-a-day guidelines, it is a by-product of soya beans (in much the same way as apple juice is to apples) and retains many of their health benefits. Yes, tofu has a mild flavour, but it is this blandness that makes it so versatile and allows it to take on the flavours of other

ONE PORTION
2–3 heaped tablespoons

ingredients. For me, marinating is a must – not only will this adds heaps of flavour but certain ingredients such as honey or maple syrup give a glossy, crisp coating. Cut the tofu into cubes or slices and marinate in curry paste, Chinese black bean, yellow bean or teriyaki sauce, oil, herbs or spices. Grate firm tofu and use it to add substance to burgers and rissoles or instead of meat in a bolognese, stir-fry, stew or curry. Ready-marinated or smoked tofu are good barbecued or roasted.

Tempeh is similar to tofu but retains more of the whole bean and has a nutty, slightly mushroomy flavour. It can be used in much the same way as tofu.

Researchers have found that soya beans and soya by-products could reduce harmful cholesterol in the body by as much as 35–40 per cent. Soya beans are also the richest source of isoflavones, a type of plant oestrogen that protects against some forms of cancer and promotes bone health. Tofu and tempeh are a good source of calcium, magnesium, phosphorus, iron, zinc, some B vitamins and vitamin E.

Maximize the nutrients

If buying fresh tofu, make sure it smells fresh and is covered with water. When you get home, change the water, store in the fridge and use within four days. Packaged tofu comes in a sealed bag containing water, which does not require changing. If cooking soya beans, follow the same guidelines as for other dried beans (see page 117) to preserve nutrient levels.

HOW TO EAT MORE...

- *Add cooked soya beans to home-made or ready-made ratatouille.*
- *Blend silken tofu with bananas and strawberries, sweeten with honey or maple syrup and dilute with milk to make a tasty, nutritious smoothie.*
- *Slice or cube smoked tofu and make a salad with shredded carrot, white cabbage, spring onions and egg noodles. Dress with a toasted sesame oil, olive oil, soy sauce and crushed garlic dressing.*
- *Marinate cubes of tofu in balsamic vinegar, honey, olive oil, orange juice and plenty of herbs for at least 1 hour. Thread onto wooden skewers and grill until golden. Serve with a tomato salsa or garlic dip.*
- *Add diced tofu to a vegetable soup, then blend once cooked until smooth and creamy.*
- *Grate firm tofu or tempeh and mix with a Thai or Indian curry paste, add enough flour to form the mixture into patties. Chill for 30 minutes then fry the patties until golden.*

GOLDEN CHINESE TOFU WITH NOODLES

Marinated black bean tofu is a firm favourite in our house. When the tofu is roasted, it develops a glossy, crisp outer coating but is still soft inside.

SERVES 4

- 325 g/11½ oz firm tofu or tempeh
- 1 tbsp sunflower oil, plus extra for oiling
- 250 g/9 oz small broccoli florets
- 1 large red pepper, seeded and sliced
- 200 g/7 oz sugar snap peas
- 2 bulbs pak choi, halved lengthways and sliced
- 1 clove garlic, finely chopped
- 100 ml/3½ fl oz fresh orange juice
- 1 tbsp soy sauce
- 250 g/9 oz egg noodles
- salt
- sesame seeds, to serve

Marinade:
- 1 clove garlic, thinly sliced
- 2 tsp fresh root ginger, peeled and grated
- 2 tsp runny honey
- 1 tbsp soy sauce
- 1 tsp toasted sesame oil
- 250 g/9 oz jar black bean sauce

1 Pat the tofu dry with kitchen towel then cut into cubes. Mix together the ingredients for the marinade in a shallow dish. Add the tofu and carefully turn it in the marinade until coated. Leave to marinate for at least 1 hour, turning occasionally.

2 Preheat the oven to 180°C/ 350°F. Place the tofu, reserving the marinade, on a lightly oiled baking sheet and roast for

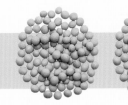

about 25 minutes, turning halfway, until crisp and golden.

3 Meanwhile, heat the oil in a wok then add the broccoli and stir-fry for 3 minutes, then add the pepper, sugar snap peas, pak choi and garlic and stir-fry for another 2 minutes.

4 Meanwhile, cook the noodles following the instructions on the packet.

5 Pour the orange juice, soy sauce and reserved marinade into the wok and stir-fry until the sauce has thickened and the vegetables are just tender.

6 Divide the noodles between four bowls, spoon over the vegetables and any sauce. Place the tofu on top and sprinkle with sesame seeds before serving.

SOYA BEAN NIBBLES

These golden, crunchy snacks make a healthy, tasty alternative to salt- and fat-laden crisps and nuts. You can also scatter them over stir-fries, salads and stews.

SERVES 15

- 225 g/8 oz dried soya beans
- 1½ tbsp soy sauce
- 2 tsp runny honey
- 2 tsp toasted sesame oil
- 1 tsp sunflower oil

1 Pick over the soya beans and remove any damaged or shrivelled ones. Put the beans in a large bowl and pour over plenty of cold water. Leave to soak overnight.

2 Drain and rinse the beans well under cold running water and put them in a large saucepan. Cover with plenty of fresh cold water and bring to a boil.

Allow to boil for 5 minutes, scooping up any white foam that rises to the surface.

3 Reduce the heat and simmer, adding more water if necessary, for about 2 hours, until tender. Drain well and leave to cool.

4 Preheat the oven to 160°C/ 325°F. Mix together the soy sauce, honey and oils in a bowl. Add the beans and stir until they are coated in the marinade. Pour the beans onto a baking sheet and roast in the oven for about 25–30 minutes until dark golden. Leave to cool slightly before eating.

Carroll & Brown would like to thank:

Design: Emily Cook, Laura de Grasse
Additional Photography: Roger Dixon
www.thinkvegetables.co.uk: MW Mack
IT Management: Paul Stradling
Proofreader: Alison Mackonochie
Index: Madeline Weston
Picture Research: Sandra Schneider

Picture Credits
Getty Images 5, 7, 44, 58, 66